SUSSEX SHIPPING
Sail, Steam & Motor
Michael Langley

MP Middleton Press

Cover pictures:

Top left -   The 1860 built brig EBERNEZER is at Arundel c1910.
Top right -   SS CLIFF QUAY, built 1950, and MV KINDRENCE, built 1976, are seen at
                  Southwick in 1983.
Porthole inset - PT EARL OF WINDSOR / RX104 built in 1867, seen at Rye, c1890.
Lower -   Fast ferry SUPERSEACAT ONE, built in 1997, manouevring astern into
                  Newhaven Harbour in 2002

To all those who have been, or are,
involved with ships and shipping- we are
still an island Nation, and forever will
depend on seaborne trade.

About the Author -

Born and bred at Horsham, West Sussex, an inkling of interest in matters nautical probably
stemmed from regular paddle steamer and early car ferry trips cross-Solent to the other family
origination point, the Isle of Wight. From the age of twelve, the much lamented Steyning line
push-pull steam train afforded visits to the Shoreham area, and a simple camera became
indispensable. On completion of the school years, a further one ensued at Navigation School,
leading to an apprenticeship as a Navigating Cadet with the P & O Group's, Trident Tankers Ltd.
A Masters Certificate was obtained in 1975, but eventually transfer to shore based employment
beckoned. This continued in ocean-going Ship Management until the early 1990s. Now residing
on the Isle of Wight, the author maintains close links with Sussex, and a 'slightly' more modern
camera continues to be on hand.

Published February 2004

ISBN 1 904474 23 3

Design   Deborah Esher
              David Pede
Typesetting   Barbara Mitchell

Published by
              Middleton Press
              Easebourne Lane
              Midhurst, West Sussex
              GU29 9AZ
Tel: 01730 813169
Fax: 01730 812601
Email: info@middletonpress.co.uk
www.middletonpress.co.uk

Printed & bound by MPG Books Ltd, Bodmin, Cornwall

CONTENTS

PREFACE

Much has been written over the years about 'Sussex by the Sea'. The aim of this book is to attempt to capture the evolution of the ships themselves, never speedier than in the 20th. century.

Accelerating industrial change together with new trading patterns, spawned new ship types, and larger individual units, in the growing search for economy of operation.

Before about 1850 wooden sailing ships had only evolved incrementally in terms of type, rigging and size. The arrival of steam power challenged the old order fundamentally.

A short geographical review of the ports is included as natural phenomena largely were responsible for their current layout. Man will always have to struggle to keep the sea out of Sussex, or put conversely, keep Sussex out of the sea.

GLOSSARY and ABBREVIATIONS

—	Sailing Ships/unpowered craft	ST	Steam Tug/Steam Tanker
PS	Paddle Steamer	TSS	Twin Screw Steamer
PT	Paddle Tug	MT	Motor Tanker/Motor Tug
SS	Steam Ship	MV	Motor Vessel

Note: from picture no.151 the pre-fix 'MV' is dropped as all subsequent ships described herein were motor powered.

Tonnages:
Net Registered Tonnage, is abbreviated to **reg. tons**
Earlier sailing ship criteria for measuring hold capacity-original derivation from 'tuns'- barrel capacity.

Gross Registered Tonnage, is abbreviated to **grt.**
Volumetric measure of enclosed space applied to all ships- i.e. 100 cu.ft. = 1 gross ton.

Deadweight Tonnage, is abbreviated to **dwt.**
An indication of the carrying capacity of the vessel in tons. This does include fuel, stores etc.

Length overall	Measurement to the fore and aft extremities
Beam or breadth	Measurement to the widest extremity

Note: in paddle steamers the recorded beam often only referred to the ship's hull - the actual width over the Paddle boxes being doubled.

Horse Power, engines:
SHP	Shaft horse power	(usually given in steamships)
BHP	Brake horse power	(usually given in motorships)

Knots: speed in nautical miles/hour.

SUSSEX PORTS MAP

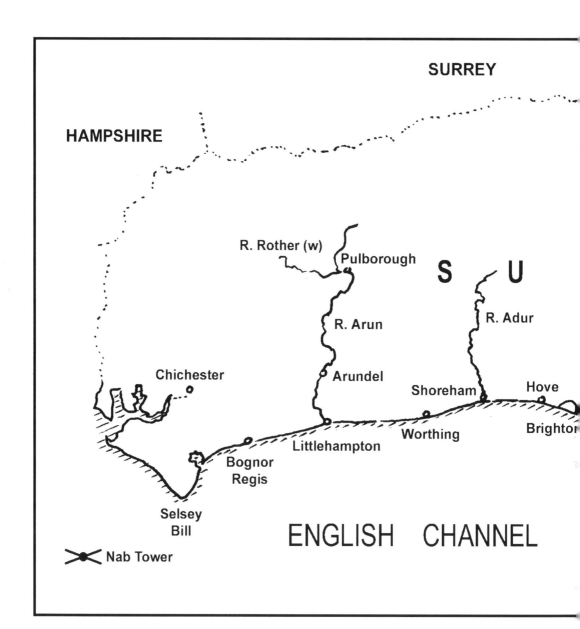

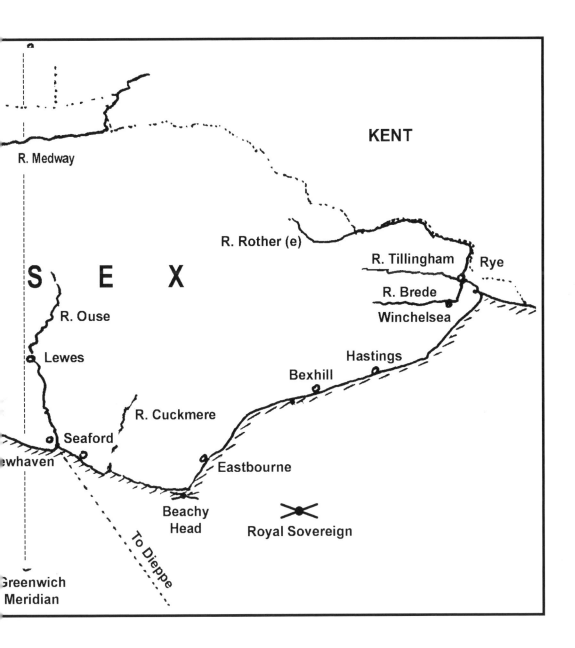

KENT

R. Medway

R. Rother (e)

R. Tillingham   Rye

S   E   X

R. Brede

R. Ouse

Winchelsea

Lewes

Hastings

Bexhill

R. Cuckmere

Seaford

whaven

Eastbourne

Beachy
Head

Royal Sovereign

To Dieppe

Greenwich
Meridian

INTRODUCTION

THE PORTS

Before examining the myriad of craft seen in the Sussex ports over the last century or so, some geographical background may be of interest. There are some striking similarities shared, and one or two features unique. All were plagued historically by wandering river mouths.

All four ports have long suffered from littoral drift, continuous tidal shift of shingle from west to east along the Channel shore. This for centuries periodically blighted trade by blocking shipping channels, until the rivers cut another exit to the sea, the whole process then repeating.

In the 18th and 19th centuries man strived to constrain many 'wayward' river mouths within fixed limits. Only the development of steam powered dredging and piling machinery ultimately achieved that goal. Basic harbour entrances could then be kept clear for shipping and trade.

Having achieved a situation where shipping may operate successfully, it can, of course, only continue to do so by dint of regular dredging. All the Sussex rivers carry silt downstream which drops out as it nears the sea, and the old enemy of shingle-drift does its best to 'bar' the entrances, as indeed it always has.

Journeying from west to east:

The River Arun, vigorous flowing in nature, passes through the South Downs gap at Arundel, but originally meandered to an exit several miles east of its present location at Littlehampton.

At Shoreham the Adur similarly cuts through the Downs gap a mile or two inland, but previously widened into a largely unprotected estuary.

In East Sussex, the Ouse, on departing Lewes, again cuts through the Downs, but once decanted to the sea at Seaford and not Newhaven.

Rye, the easternmost port, had also been sited on a large estuary but when the River Brede to Winchelsea silted, the latter's trade vanished to the benefit of Rye. Ultimately, the combined flow of the Rivers Tillingham and Rother left a channel where once the estuary prevailed miles inland. The sea is now a couple of miles from Rye Town, and half a mile from Rye Harbour village.

Shoreham and Rye have shared centuries of varying fortunes in both shipbuilding and trade, largely either boom or bust, often quite simply dictated by irregular access to or from the sea.

Littlehampton and Newhaven's prosperity is more recent, respectively advancing on the decline of Arundel and Lewes, as ports.

CHICHESTER HARBOUR

Chichester Ship Canal had become commercially disused before the First World War. Only a few hundred tons of cargo were carried annually by the 1890s. The small dimensions to which the canal's 'Salterns' entrance lock had been constructed precluded all but the tiniest commercial craft of the day.

In ship terms, 90ft length by 18ft 6in beam and approx 5ft draught allowed only for the passage of tiny brigs, ketches and barges with a capacity of about 100 tons of cargo. Operations on this minor scale soon became commercially unviable, given the direct competition with the Railway Yards at Chichester.

Today, the Canal is being rejuvenated for leisure use by the Chichester Ship Canal Trust.

ARUNDEL and LITTLEHAMPTON

The River Arun finally was tamed into its present 'outlet' in about 1735 at Littlehampton. Ships over 100 tons could then reach Arundel on the tide, given the improved river channel. Similar sized vessels were built at Arundel, just below the bridge, but by the mid-1800s larger wooden ocean trading barques, brigs etc., up to 500 tons were coming off the Clymping slipways, at Littlehampton. The arrival of the railway and wharf at this location allowed access for larger vessels and to some extent obviated the 'haul' upriver to Arundel, where seagoing traffic ended by World War I.

SHOREHAM

From the 13th to the 19th century, the River Adur's course was particularly mobile of habit. The wide open estuary developed a spit which grew relentlessly eastwards, almost from Lancing to Hove. At various locations, in turn, the river would break through to the sea, giving periodic access for shipping.

Strangely, the present harbour mouth at Kingston, lies approximately in the middle of the

Adur's wanderings, this of course after much piling and dredging rendered a usable and navigable entrance. With the construction in 1855 of Southwick Lock, the one and a half miles of old river bed to Aldrington, became the Ship Canal. This remains the only useful enclosed dock in Sussex, allowing ships to remain afloat at all times. Shoreham has thereafter much benefitted as a busy port.

In Elizabethan time, Shoreham's shipbuilders turned out 'Men-of-War', and trading vessels for the East India Company, ships up to 400 tons. When local wooden shipbuilding ceased in the 1880s, 800 ton barques were coming off the slips. Henceforth, iron and steel hulled vessels prevailed, but not from Sussex shipyards.

The arrival of the railway at Kingston Wharf brought more trade. However, tight track curves and an inclined plane to the main line was very restrictive, only the shortest wheelbase wagons and lightest shunting engines could be employed. Initially wagons were winched up to the main line sidings.

LEWES and NEWHAVEN

From its mouth at Seaford, the Sussex Ouse had long been navigable by small seagoing vessels up to Lewes. Becoming choked, the Ouse mouth shifted back westwards to Meeching, a village that was destined to become Newhaven. Further channel re-aligning improved river flow and general accessibility, for example North quay opposite Denton Island.

Shipbuilding developed at Newhaven from the 1700s, brigs and barques up to about 500 tons being launched. Lewes itself had a smaller ship-building industry in the mid 1800s, producing craft up to about 100 tons.

The mid 1800s saw the arrival, in a big way, of the London, Brighton and South Coast Railway, which transformed Newhaven into a very well connected rail port, serving the Cross-Channel and other trades.

RYE and RYE HARBOUR

The large estuary already described dwindled rapidly, leaving the Rother, Brede and Tillingham to channel to the sea. Periodically a great storm shifted the river mouth, then in the 18th century much effort and manpower attempted to constrain matters. The sea itself on occasion undid these works in short order, and it was in the 1920s that training walls and groynes finally

harnessed the river mouth to its present site. The silty river and inevitable bar will always require remedial action to maintain a navigable channel.

Rye's shipyards were sometimes very prolific over the centuries building wooden ocean trading vessels up to about 300 tons, and a wide range of coastal and fishing types, launched as and when the river depths allowed.

Rye also benefitted from the arrival of a goods branch line to Rye Harbour, in 1854 (South Eastern Railway).

THE SHIPS

Sailing vessels, wooden in construction, carried men and materials for thousands of years. Coal fired, steam powered, wooden ships soon proliferated in the early 1800s progressing to iron then steel hulls. By the 1900s the days of ocean trading sailing ships were numbered, to be followed a few decades later by the last coastal commercial 'sailers'.

Also early in the 20th century, basic 'oil' engines appeared, soon developing into the more sophisticated, and now universal, motorships. The last oil fired steam powered coastal craft appeared in the 1950s, but were largely extinct by the 1980s, unable to compete on manpower or fuel costs with the new motorships.

At the start of the 21st century, it is difficult to conjecture the next propulsive force, other than increasingly efficient variations of similar motors.

Utilising many unseen and some rarely seen photographs, we examine that diversity of craft seen in or around the Sussex ports over the last 100 years. Some visited once, some occasionally, others hundreds of times, and a few became permanent fixtures. A few early examples built in Sussex survived long enough to make it well into the 20th century, a wonderful testament to Sussex shipyards and shipwrights of old, and to Sussex timber.

Where it is known, precise photograph dates are given, otherwise the best possible approximation is shown. Photographic sources are listed at the end and, as a mark of respect to those pioneers, where available, names included.

In these days of 'political correctness' ships are deemed to be neuter, but anyone who has ever been involved with the operation of ships will know otherwise - in the seafarer's time honoured way, in this book ships are 'female'.

Naturally, in sailing ship days, everything was manually operated, crews were large and navigational equipment somewhat rudimentary, magnetic compass, a hand lead and a few old charts with the enormous hard-won skill of master and crew. Some of the brigs, schooners, ketches and barges lasted many decades, others came to grief quickly, not able to beat their way off a leeshore or evade grounding or a collision in fog.

Even some of the best run steamers continued to fall foul of similar disasters until the post World War II universal spread and development of radar, reached all merchant shipping in the subsequent decades. The radio direction finding equipment helped too, along with the now outmoded Decca Navigator system. Now, with satellite based global positioning universally available, pin-point accuracy is the rule, whatever the weather. Coming to grief is now mercifully rare.

The ships themselves tend to fall into several categories or types according to trade involvement. Some converted from one role to another as economics dictated. Around our coasts coal was king for centuries, general cargo, timber carrier, passenger ferry, oil tanker, sand dredger, tug, etc, all distinct and evolving designs. By the end of the 20th.century, wine tanker, mini-bulker, roll-on roll-off, container ships and superfast ferries, survey ships, to name but a few, were added.

Dry cargo carrying ships were traditionally fitted with derricks for working cargo, this tended to be superseded by gearless ships reliant on shore cranes for loading and discharge. Recently, trends are more in favour of ship's gear yet again, and deck mounted excavators from shore applications are finding their way afloat, thus rendering some vessels' geared.

Individual ship units are now much larger than just a few years ago, this also in the never ending search for economy of operation. Sadly, this has seen the demise of many once thriving small wharves, and harbour facilities, converting to yacht marinas and residential accommodation.

Coasters of thousands of tons have replaced those of but a few hundred.

If we permit ourselves a short 'time-warp' back 100 years - what would those old boys, tacking a coal brig in a gale towards port, have said if a 38 knot high speed monohull ferry had rocketed past? Probably something entirely unprintable.

The book aims to blend factual ship development and evolution with nostalgia unashamedly.

The earliest dated photograph is 1887, the most recent 2003.

The earliest ship build date is 1856, the most recent is 2001.

A list of publications recommended for further reading and research is included at the end.

Notes:

Fishing vessels are omitted herein; for they are a massive subject in their own right.

Attempting to cover four ports and large numbers of ships unequally distributed between them has been a little problematical. The readers forbearance is sought, as he seemingly flits from one end of Sussex to the other. There is, however, an intended rationale in the build dates of the ships themselves, their evolution being the main theme. Photograph dates may similarly confuse, due to the extreme longevity of certain vessels; hopefully all will clarify as we sail, steam or motor ahead.

The maps will hopefully assist the reader to 'navigate' the Sussex rivers and coast from the comfort of an armchair. It's time to stoke up that 'galley-range' and make tea.

THE MAPS

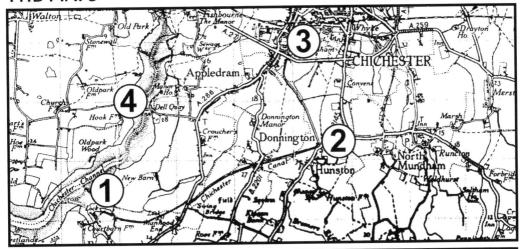

No.1. Map: Chichester Harbour

(1)   Salterns Lock, provided access to/from the canal via the Chichester Harbour Channel, to the Sea.

(2)   The Canal branch to Southgate Basin, in the City, diverged from the track of the old Portsmouth to Arundel Canal at Hunston.

(3)   Southgate Basin - Chichester's own dock.

(4)   Dell Quay, 2 miles from the City and on the tidal channel continued in commercial use until World War II. This too subsequently became outmoded by the increasing size of ships, and growth in the road haulage industry.

No.2. Map: The River Arun, Arundel to Littlehampton

(1)   Site of Arundel's seagoing trade below the road bridge which represented the limit of seagoing navigation. The commercial wharves were, along with the last shipyard, on the town bank although in earlier centuries, barge docks had been cut into the opposite bank. Barge traffic upriver of Arundel ceased c.1930.

(2)   Ford Railway Bridge, originally an imposing wooden drawbridge structure, had been replaced in 1862 by an iron one, of lift and side slide operation. This was strengthened in 1898, and replaced in 1938 with the present fixed steel span.

(3)   The Railway Wharf, Littlehampton Town, is the farthest upstream commercial wharf in the harbour. Latterly accessible through the 1908 swingbridge, and even more recently, the retractable footbridge. Just below, on the west bank, Harveys' Shipyard and slipways were in business.

No. 3 Map: The River Adur, Shoreham

(1)   Limit of Navigation: road and rail bridges across the Adur from Shoreham town. River barge traffic from Beeding Cement Works, a couple of miles upstream, ceased in about 1929.

(2)   Site of the Railway Company's Wharf and 1860s cross channel services etc; Also the 'ultimate' mouth of the Adur. Kingston.

(3)   Southwick Locks: 1855, 1933, 1957, the Canal thence running to Aldrington Basin, Hove, being deepened in 1933 and again in the 1950's redevelopments.

(4)   Site of progressive gas/electricity works installations from east to west, from 1870 to the present.

(5)   Hove Boating Lagoon, site of the Adur's most easterly exit to the sea, created from marshland by Hove Council in about 1931.

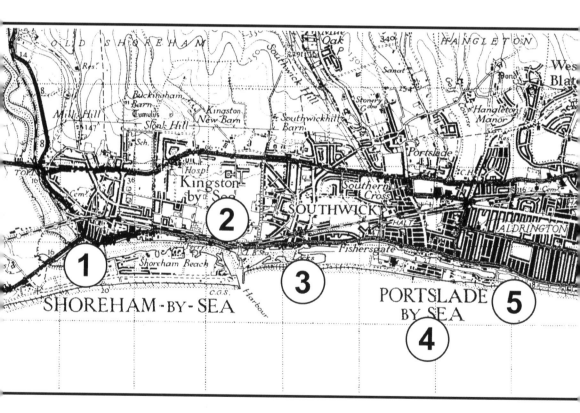

Maps 1 to 5 are based on the 1946 Ordnance Survey edition of 1946.

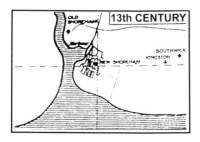

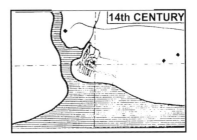

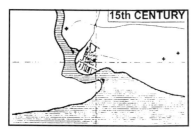

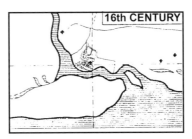

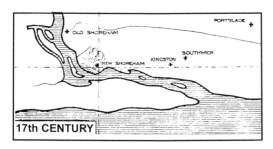

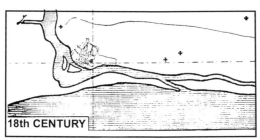

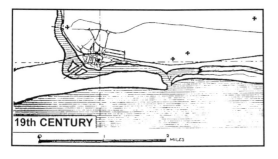

The Adur's advance

13th & 14th CENTURY

The harbour, exposed from the south, lies between New and Old Shoreham. The dotted lines reference to one fixed point - the Church.

15th CENTURY

Littoral drift has started to shape the shingle spit to the eastwards.

16th & 17th CENTURY

The spit's progress has been phenomenal, causing shoaling and even temporary islands to develop in the shallow river bed.

18th CENTURY

Having reached Hove and made numerous exits to the sea en route, the Adur finally exits at Kingston.

19th CENTURY & beyond

The 1855 lock at Southwick forms the access to The Canal the remaining 'abandoned' bed of the river, to Aldrington Basin. Also, Shoreham Beach had acquired its basic shape.

(maps: sources various but co-ordinated in 1921 by H. Cheal, Shoreham)

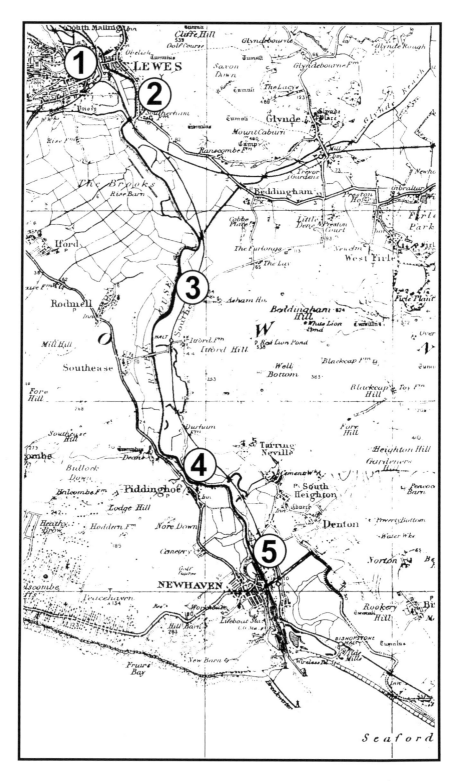

← No.4. Map: The River Ouse, Lewes to Newhaven

(1)   Cliffe Bridge, Lewes, had commercial wharves both above and below for seagoing vessels. River barge traffic upriver from Lewes had ceased long before the last seagoing barges visited the town, c.1938.

(2)   Southerham Quay: cement traffic exported up to 1934.

(3)   Asham Cement Works Quay: active 1934-1967 cement exports. Commercial shipping above Newhaven ceased on its closure.

(4)   Piddinghoe: Every's Wharf, handled iron products and some scrap cargoes before the early 1950s closure. Clay Dock: clay barged upriver to cement works.

(5)   North Quay, Newhaven, still active commercially and the seagoing limit for such vessels.

No.5. Map: Rye & Rye Harbour.

Rivers, Brede, Tillingham and Rother

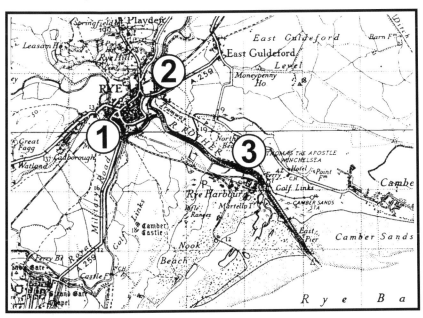

(1)   Strand Quay River Tillingham, Rye Town. Road bridge and river sluice form the limit of seagoing navigation. River barge traffic above Rye ceased c.1928

(2)   River Rother, road and rail bridges above the Fishmarket limit the navigation. Barge traffic above here ceased by early 1930s.

(3)   Rye Harbour. Commercial wharf still active; built 1967

SHIPS
by date of build

1. SUSSEX MAID

Built by Gray of Newhaven in 1856 as a brig (square rigged on both masts) for Lewes owners Chatfield, here seen moored on the left of the photo, she traded widely before rerigging as a more handy, less labour intensive, brigantine in the 1870's. G.Robinson of Newhaven then operated her in the coal trade until he died in 1903, when the old ship was sold. This photograph is readily dateable as the paddle steamer *PS SOUTHAMPTON* alongside came briefly to operate from Newhaven in 1902. Registered in her namesake port, the 1872 built paddle steamer had been a product of Barclay, Curle, Glasgow for Red Funnel, and had just completed 30 years service on their Southampton-Cowes route. Capable of 12 knots and with a capacity for 272 passengers, at 150ft length by 20ft beam she was a typical, rather narrow-gutted, Victorian paddler of the day. Seemingly, the Newhaven operation was none too successful, as soon a brief period in foreign ownership ensued before a further career with the Liverpool and North Wales SS Co. as *St. Eilian* kept her away from the scrapyard until 1915.

2. EBERNEZER

This fine old brigantine, another re-rigged brig, started life in 1860 at the Shoreham shipyard of May. Of 177 reg. tons she could carry 300 tons of cargo on a draught of 11ft length and breadth being 109ft by 26ft 6 in. Briefly part of the Stephenson, Clarke fleet, she was sold on for further trading to J.Robinson of Littlehampton, in 1895, frequently bringing coal to her home port and Arundel until sold in 1915. *Ebernezer* became a war loss off Dieppe in 1917. The c.1910 photograph shows her moored on a misty day at Arundel Gas Company's Wharf, about to discharge her cargo of coal in the time honoured way of man, wheelbarrow, and stout gangplank. One can only ponder whether, on occasion, man, wheelbarrow and coal went 'mudwards'! A charming tale from the period prevails whereby on turning the ship ready for the trip back down river, *Ebernezer's* bowsprit decapitated a nearby cottage chimney pot - surely an amusing incident except for the irate cottage dweller. In a career spanning 57 years rather more good fortune than bad luck must have blessed *Ebernezer*.

3. SARAH

Another brigantine from May's Shoreham Shipyard, *Sarah* followed *Ebernezer* to Littlehampton's Robinson fleet in 1896, remaining until 1910. The photograph of the harbour tug *Jumna* towing the *Sarah* to sea in front of a fascinated crowd of onlookers in about 1908 has been seen many times before. However no apology is made for reproducing it here as it wonderfully captures the last days of coastal sail. Within another five or six years, *Sarah* and few remaining vessels of her type, and indeed, the *Jumna*, had gone, steam and auxiliary powered craft having taken over. By the direction of two visible wind vanes, *Sarah*, crew rapidly making sail, will have a favourable start to her trip back to the North - East Coast. *Sarah* was built in 1862.

4. AMANDA →

Built at Portmadoc, and seen here beneath the East Sussex cliffs, *Amanda* was latterly engaged in George Robinson's coal trade to Newhaven up to 1903, thence sold on only to be lost in 1905. In the photograph, not a stitch of sail has been lowered and as *Amanda* is evidently loaded she must be about to tack toward the harbour entrance. Considering the punishing nature of coastal trade, it is a huge endorsement of the skills of captains and crews, that so many of these old timers lasted so many decades. Captain Richard Robinson of the *Amanda* later became a pilot at Newhaven.

5. PT EARL OF WINDSOR/RX104 →

At 79grt, this wooden hulled steam paddle tug dated from 1867, The '*Earl*' had already spent twenty years in general towage work in the Firth of Forth area of Scotland. In 1888 she appeared at Rye and, rather uniquely for her type, became a registered fishing vessel in the local fleet. Fitted with a derrick, no doubt she became a versatile tug indeed for Owners Hoads, who seemingly only kept her for a couple of years, selling back to Fife for £350. The photograph therefore is c.1890. Perhaps the shoaling waterways and limited manoeuvring space in Rye's channels had some bearing on her short stay. Rye, had historically, seen hundreds of smacks, cutters, ketches and even a few steam trawlers built at several now long defunct shipyards.

6. PS GLEN ROSA

The 1877 built *Glen Rosa* worked several locations in the Victorian and Edwardian paddler excursion steamer era. In this pre WWI scene she is operating along the Sussex Coast for Campbells, and as one of the smaller units of that fleet she would call at some of the less accessible piers barred to her bigger sister vessels. The ship is of typical 1870s design with the inevitable open bridge abaft the funnel. The after deck on this steamer had no saloon structure at all, patrons being afforded a degree of weather protection from a full width stretched canvas awning cover. Another feature much seen in early paddlers was a staysail rigged and ready for action if necessary.

7. PT STELLA & SISSIE

Built in 1879 the 76 ton paddle tug *Stella* is a good example of a harbour tug of the day, nevertheless quite capable of mounting towage and rescue operations in the English Channel. Such duties were not uncommon in the latter days of sailing traders. In fact steam tugs had seen progressive use throughout the 1800s beginning with wooden hulls, but soon progressing to iron c.1840 and steel together with the new screw propulsion a few decades later. *Stella* operated at Shoreham for the Harbour Trustees over several decades. The photograph shows her berthed just outside the 1855 lock at Southwick, no doubt ready for the day's work, being salvage of a stricken craft or towing mud hoppers to sea. Steam is up - there's a shimmer at the top of the funnel. A 382grt steel hulled motor schooner of Dutch origins, *Sissie,* is just running a line to the lock wall, courtesy of the boatman or 'huffler' as they were always known at Shoreham. Although still setting a full set of fore and aft sails, the 1919 built *Sissie* would largely rely on her oil engine for manoeuvring and passage making in adverse winds.

←8. PT JUMNA

The *Jumna* appears to have been almost legendary of fame, as she busily towed sailing ships in and out of Littlehampton, and to and from Arundel, several miles up the River Arun. Owned by C.H.Campbell, she could be closely observed by the Victorian and Edwardian trippers on the pier at Littlehampton, also by those intrepid early photographers. In quiet ship towage times *Jumna* would see duty as a 'trippers' steamer, out round the bay. Finally, c.1914 and with the general demise of the last coal brigs, and the virtual end of Arundel's seaborne traffic, she was sold on to the Middle East for further service. *Jumna* dated from 1884 and measured 51grt. Steam coasters brought her career to an end, at least on the Arun, after thirty years work. In the photograph c.1905, *Jumna* has just turned a coal brigantine off the berth at Arundel - the Castle visible between tug and tow and they are stoking up the boiler for the trip back down river to Littlehampton, and the sea.

↙9. SS GANNET

An iron hulled steamer of 263grt, measuring 133ft by 22ft by 11ft; the iron rope guard across the poop indicates that *Gannet* could if required, engage in towing operations. The 1930s photograph shows her well moored (partly by chains) on the south side of Aldrington Basin, Hove. Note the complete lack of quayside development. *Gannet* was built at Hull in 1884 and was owned in 1934 by Henry Burden of Poole.

10. ALERT

This attractive little three masted schooner is the *Alert*, 133 reg.tons, and Truro owned in the 1930s. She was built at Runcorn in 1885. Large numbers of this type existed, some trading up to as late as the 1950s, given some auxiliary engine power. The series of photographs date from the early 1930s, and here record a voyage to Newhaven and up the River Ouse.

10.1 With flying jib and mizzen taken in, *Alert* is standing toward Newhaven Breakwater, in laden condition.

10.2 Everys Wharf, Piddinghoe, a couple of miles upstream of Newhaven is the scene of discharge, probably pig iron, and a good stack appears on the quayside, overlooked by Piddinghoe Church visible between main and mizzen mast. A simple scotch derrick type crane can be seen on the right.

10.3 Now empty and probably await-ing orders, *Alert* has come back down the Ouse to the stages in Newhaven Harbour, opposite the railway quays. *Alert* was con-verted into a twin screw motor yacht in 1938, but broken up during World War II.

11.1 and 11.2 PS WORTHING BELLE

Originally a River Clyde steamer, the *Diana Vernon* came to the Sussex Coast in 1901. Brighton and Worthing piers and Littlehampton Harbour were regular haunts, the ship being Sussex owned. Built by Barclay, Curle Glasgow in 1885, *Worthing Belle* went out to Istanbul for Bosphorus ferry work on her departure from Sussex in 1914. The first photograph, not such a common view for the Littlehampton photographers, is taken from the west bank of the harbour. In the second picture the ship is evidently manouevring off one of the Sussex Piers, with a good loading of trippers onboard. The dates c.1902 and 1908.

12. ROSIE

Towards the end of wooden shipbuilding at Littlehampton (Clymping Yard), J.& W.B.Harvey built a long series of sailing, gaff or 'boomie' coastal ketches. These were of quite modest dimensions and relatively shallow draught, enabling them to carry cargoes into shallow rivers. *Rosie* of 1886 is a good example being of 78reg tons and 85ft in length by 20ft beam and 6ft draught. This particular vessel was also owned by her builders. The photograph, one of a few in the book not actually in Sussex, is included, as by chance the *Rosie* herself helped to identify and precisely date the scene. *Rosie* is working cargo at a berth just below the 1799-1889 wooden trestle bridge over the River Itchen, at Northam, Southampton. This bridge was demolished c.1890, a new iron structure replacing it. That in turn, again being replaced by the present 1954 concrete structure. Date of photograph therefore 1886-89.

13.1 and 13.2 SS PORTSLADE

The first steam collier of many to feature herein, *Portslade* was by no means her owner's first such vessel. She is an excellent example of the early type, her career with Stephenson, Clarke lasting until 1908. *Portslade* was built in 1888. Powered by a compound steam engine, the 634grt *Portslade* just fitted the 1855 Southwick Lock and could deliver 1,000 tons of coal to her namesake gasworks, per trip. The photograph, from a low quality negative, is included for its rarity as it shows the ship entering Shoreham Harbour, sail brailed into the mast, and with paddle tug in attendance astern. Note also the open wheelhouse, or rather, lack thereof. Dating from c.1905, the lower picture shows discharge underway at the Portslade Gas Works, by way of an early vertically boiled steam crane two of which were here provided. Mechanised discharge had arrived.

14. MOUNTSFIELD →

A 126 ton 'boomie" ketch, *Mountsfield* appeared in 1890, one of a series built by G.& T.Smith of Rye in an attempt to restore commercial shipping to the port, after a period of relative inactivity. The photograph, dating from c.1900, shows the ship berthed at the top end of Strand Quay, River Tillingham, Rye, ready to discharge - probably coal to waiting carts or overside to a Rother lighter for a destination upstream. Horses, carts and river lighters ruled the day. Cockbilled on the foremast, the long yard indicates *Mountsfield* could still set a large square foresail, given a following breeze. In 1919 the ship was sold on to Cardiff owners.

15. ATHOLE

Proving just how popular the 'boomie' ketches became, *Athole* was a Shoreham-built example from 1892 and is seen here at Rye Harbour c.1905, discharging (probably coal) by way of a small steam crane to railway trucks of the early round-ended type. The South Eastern Railway Company had built this branch to Rye Harbour from Rye Town in 1854. It lasted up until 1962 when the rails were removed. Alongside *Athole* can be seen the inevitable Rother lighter, loading for places upstream and across the river another boomie ketch awaits action at the stages. All around can be seen local inshore craft. No trace of this wharf exists today - the 1967 commercial wharf is just a few hundred yards, upstream.

16. JACHIN

Of 70 reg tons and built at Maldon by Howard, this coastal barge was regarded as a particularly fine 'sailer', although she had more than her fair share of maritime mishaps. *Jachin* appeared in 1893. Once abandoned mid-channel, she was found and salved by French fishermen. Also, she ran aground off Newhaven, in Seaford Bay, but again, came through the ordeal, later being rebuilt and renamed *VENTA*, finally converting to a yacht. *Jachin* would probably have carried about 120 tons of cargo, and in the photograph c.1900, can be seen in company with two other barges, just below Cliffe Bridge, Lewes - a veritable hive of industry. *Jachin*, alone in the picture, has her gear completely lowered, evidence that she had been to an upstream wharf to discharge, and now awaits the tide, to pole-off down the Ouse to Newhaven. The connecting bridge in the background was of the 'withdrawing' variety. Barges of this type were frequent visitors to Lewes until the second World War. Between the three in this scene something in the order of a not insignificant 350 tons would have been handled. For a present day comparison view see photograph - caption no. 201.

17. RESULT→

Built at Carrickfergus, N.Ireland, the steel hulled *Result* entered the water in 1893. She measured 125grt, 103ft in length and her type was three masted topsail schooner. In an incredibly long (70 years) trading career, *Result* visited most ports around the British coast. Progressively updated rigs and ever more powerful auxiliary engines, finally she traded as a motorship, reduced to ketch rig, thus competing very successfully with many a more modern motor coaster. Registered at Barnstaple, Devon, in latter years typical cargoes were coal to small West Country ports or, in the case of her Sussex visitations, lime or cement to the islands of the English Channel. On final retirement from the coasting trade, *Result* was lifted out of the water by Harland and Wolff's Belfast giant shipyard crane, and taken by road to The Ulster Folk and Transport Museum for display. *Result's* last cargo had been c.1967. In the photograph taken in the 1930s, she is laying at Newhaven's Railway Quay.

18. PADDLER POWER AT LITTLEHAMPTON

In this delightful postcard scene of about 1913 three paddlers are visible in the form of *Jumna*, *Worthing Belle* and *Albion*. This last vessel is of particular interest as she was a member of the famous P. & A. Campbell, White Funnel Fleet. The Campbell Brothers brought their operations to the Sussex Coast in 1901, from the Bristol Channel to capture the increasingly popular excursion traffic. *Albion* was an occasional performer, and in the picture is about to take the berth vacated by a well loaded *Worthing Belle*. The sun must have been shining on all. Careful examination of *Albion* reveals that in common with many other paddle steamers of the day, she had received - extra sets of lifeboat davits - regulatory change following the Titanic tragedy of 1912. *Jumna* and *Worthing Belle* had both gone by 1914, the scene must have been in carefree days just before the Military took over the ports for the duration of the War. *Albion* survived the war, serving as an Admiralty minesweeper, but sadly was broken up thereafter, being beyond repair although her engines were removed for fitting into a later paddler.

19. HETTY, PEGASUS & CENTAUR

Another industrial scene in the heart of Lewes from the early 1900s. Three spritsail rigged barges are working cargo along the wharves of the Ouse, the nearest, *Centaur*, is moored at Every's Ironworks, Phoenix Factory. Centaur, 60 reg tons, came from a Harwich yard in 1895. The furthest craft, *Hetty*, appears to have been of Dutch origins, judging by her bow and general shape, although sprit rigged. A few Dutch craft came to the British Register, and this rig. As in the earlier *Jachin* picture, a good 3/400 tons would have been shifted by these hard working little ships. Iron, coal and timber, and agricultural cargoes would have been commonplace.

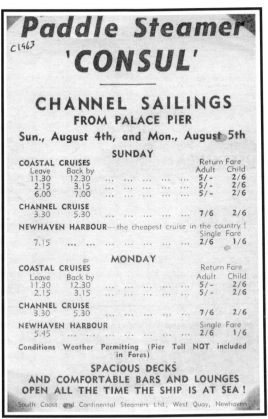

Paddle Steamer
C1463
'CONSUL'

CHANNEL SAILINGS
FROM PALACE PIER
Sun., August 4th, and Mon., August 5th

SUNDAY

COASTAL CRUISES							Return Fare	
Leave	Back by						Adult	Child
11.30	12.30	...	...	...	...	...	5/-	2/6
2.15	3.15	...	...	...	...	...	5/-	2/6
6.00	7.00	...	...	...	...	...	5/-	2/6

CHANNEL CRUISE								
3.30	5.30	...	...	...	...	...	7/6	2/6

NEWHAVEN HARBOUR—the cheapest cruise in the country !

							Single Fare	
7.15	...	...	...	...	...	...	2/6	1/6

MONDAY

COASTAL CRUISES							Return Fare	
Leave	Back by						Adult	Child
11.30	12.30	...	...	...	...	...	5/-	2/6
2.15	3.15	...	...	...	...	...	5/-	2/6

CHANNEL CRUISE								
3.30	5.30	...	...	...	...	...	7/6	2/6

NEWHAVEN HARBOUR							Single Fare	
5.45	...	...	...	...	...	...	2/6	1/6

Conditions Weather Permitting (Pier Toll NOT included in Fares)

SPACIOUS DECKS
AND COMFORTABLE BARS AND LOUNGES
OPEN ALL THE TIME THE SHIP IS AT SEA !

South Coast and Continental Steamers Ltd., West Quay, Newhaven.

20. PS CONSUL

The 277 grt *Consul*, unusually for her type, came from the London yard of R.H.Green & Co, in 1896. Of 175ft by 21ft beam she would have been more like 40ft over the paddleboxes - officialdom used not to record this measurement, which in general approximated twice the hull width. Until 1938, *Consul* was known as *Duke of Devonshire*, renaming when she joined Cosens, Weymouth fleet in 1938. By 1962 and just beginning to show her extreme age, new owners South Coast and Continental Steamers attempted to run her along the Sussex Coast from Brighton, Eastbourne etc; reliability problems and the general public's decreasing interest in such activities, meant this was not a huge success. Retirement followed. The photograph dates from a little earlier in the 1950s and the old ship is backing away from Weymouth Pier. When operating in Sussex the Consul had a plain buff funnel.

21 . PS BRIGHTON QUEEN (1)

In 1901 the Brighton, Worthing and South Coast Steamboat Company decided to sell up. P.& A.Campbell took their two widely differing paddlers into their own fleet. *Brighton Queen* was given what today might be called a complete makeover - rendering her rather unusual appearance more in line with White Funnel proportions. The other steamer, the smaller *Princess May*, went to Italy shortly after the takeover. Campbells then set about opening a regional office in Brighton, the ships operational base becoming Newhaven Harbour. Paddlers were often switched with the Bristol Channel operations. *Brighton Queen* became a huge favourite with the public, being a very good 'sea-boat' and fast enough for the longer day excursions to France. During World War I, minesweeping duties called, a chore much given to paddlers due to their shallow draught, and duly *Brighton Queen* succumbed to a mine. Note the furled staysail and lack of a wheelhouse - Campbells removed her original one - and kept their fleet a wheelhouse free zone until after World War II, for the paddlers, at least. Also noteworthy - lack of a forward pair of lifeboats - the *Titanic* had yet to 'happen'. This *Brighton Queen* was built in 1897; another paddler, the *Lady Moyra* was given the name in 1933 and that ship had two funnels.

22.1 PS BRIGHTON BELLE
Seen approaching Hastings Pier in the 1930's is the 1900 built 320grt. paddler *Brighton Belle*. This ship had originally sailed under the name of *Lady Evelyn*.

22.2 PS BRIGHTON QUEEN (2)
The 1905 built ship had been named *Gwalia* and ran for the Barry Railway Company at first. Later she went to Tuckers of Cardiff as *Lady Moyra*, before joining the Campbell fleet. From 1933 the 807grt twin funnelled steamer became the second *Brighton Queen* and easily distinguishable in the fleet by her square upper deck ports. Both these ships attended Dunkirk but were subsequently lost in that campaign.

←23. EVELYN

G.& T. Smith of Rye built this ketch in 1900, *Evelyn* joined the local fleet of George Coote who also owned trawlers. Reportedly, her Master was Captain Coffin.The coal and general trades would have been bread and butter for the *Evelyn*. In the photograph the ship looks immaculate, possibly reflecting a recent entry into trade and indeed, the water. *Evelyn* measured 99grt.

↙24. CONVOY

From the same yard at Rye in 1900 came the *Convoy*, 100grt. She was a coastal sailing barge type, and is a good example of how many a sailer was given a new lease of life by conversion to a full motor powered vessel. *Convoy* for many years belonged to Sullys and was registered at Dover. She motored on in the coastal and estuarial trades right up to the 1970's, and indeed is still afloat today. A great credit to G.& T.Smith, the quality of Sussex timber and careful owners. The delightful aerial study from the 1950's shows just how smart a barge she was- clean and tidy throughout and seemingly still, on occasion, setting a foresail.

25. SIX SISTERS

Built at Kalmar, Sweden in 1902, the 169 grt *Six Sisters* had an unusual end to her career. A typical Scandinavian timber built three masted schooner, in the early 1930s she had arrived at Hull with a timber cargo. The owners defaulted and she lay for some years with a writ nailed to the mast, this under her previous name *Sigrid*. Subsequently she resumed trading as *Six Sisters*, finding her way to Sussex by World War II. Ultimately, she was moored mid-canal at Fishersgate between the Shoreham gasworks and electricity works, as a deterrent to any enemy seaplanes with a mind to land thereabouts. Vandalism, fire and general obsolescence lead to final scrapping locally, after the War.

Note: The photograph, dated Shoreham Harbour 1940, does not actually properly identify the ship; if any reader can confirm, the author would be pleased to 'be put straight'.

26.1 SS PORTSMOUTH

The combined French and British operation on the Newhaven-Dieppe route added *SS Portsmouth* to the fleet in 1902. This vessel was of 530grt 204ft in length by 26ft beam, and had been built at Le Havre. She carried the French flag. All forms of general cargo were the preserve of this type of ship running in parallel to the faster passenger steamers. *Portsmouth* was fitted with the normal triple expansion engines and served the route for her owners until 1935. The postcard view c.1910 clearly shows sailing coasters to be much in evidence, however further up the Railway Quay towards the massive sheerlegs, an Isle of Wight paddler is in for maintenance, beyond the local tug.

26.2 ST ALERT

Seen towing a small brigantine to sea at Newhaven, c.1903 is the railway company harbour tug *Alert*. Dating from 1898, this 175grt steamer operated for about three decades out of Newhaven. In the photograph *Alert* appears to dwarf the little brigantine, which, judging by the calm conditions is about to go 'nowhere fast' once the tow rope has been dropped. This kind of tug work was drawing to a close at this period as steam and motor ships steadily displaced the remaining 'sailers'.

27.1 and 27.2 CELTIC

This barge had first been a member of E.J.&W.Goldsmiths' large fleet, the steel hulled types being nicknamed 'ironpots'. *Celtic* and some of her sister barges came from Dutch yards, in this case Papendrecht. In photograph (1) *Celtic* is in original spritsail rig condition and yet to receive a motor. She was built in 1903. 153 grt 90ft by 23ft and 8ft draught, and could carry about 230 tons of cargo. When Asham Cement Works opened on the River Ouse, a few miles upstream of Newhaven, Goldsmith sailing and motor barges were regular visitors as coal for the works and export cement cargoes started to flow. Coal often came from Dover and cement went to the Channel Islands and coastal destinations such as the Isle of Wight. Photograph (2) from the top of Newhaven's sheerlegs, shows *Celtic* en-route to Asham, c.1960, to load. In 1941 twin 3cyl oil engines rendered her a fully powered motor barge. Shortly after World War II, Capt.Alf Sheaf from the Isle of Wight purchased *Celtic*, thereafter the old ship traded from the River Ouse to the River Medina, I.O.W., carrying thousands of tons of cement over the years until Asham Works closed in 1967. Cement then went to the Isle of

Wight from (briefly) Shoreham, then Greenhithe. In 1969 *Celtic* retired to be replaced by the ex Dutch coaster *Dina*, renamed *Ash Lake*. *Celtic* still exists, partly restored at a Thames Estuary barge museum.

27.3
Celtic is loading bagged cement at Asham 1962.

27.4
Retired - Newport Quay, I.O.W. in around 1970.

28. NEWHAVEN HARBOUR SWINGBRIDGE

In 1866, to replace an earlier structure, this iron swingbridge was brought into service, to carry the main Sussex coast road over the River Ouse, and to support a rail connection to the Company's sidings at West Quay and the harbour mouth. Careful examination of No. 27 *Celtic*, photograph 2, shows the rail track to be on the south side of the bridge roadway. Any vessel wishing to proceed to the North Quay, Piddinghoe, Asham, or up to Lewes had of course, to await the opening 'gang', whose manual cranking caused some delay to ever increasing motor traffic levels. After not inconsiderable local difficulty, a modern replacement swingbridge finally materialised c.1974. The West Quay sidings had already been abandoned, so no rail link was provided across the new bridge.The Postcard c.1920 is from the London Brighton & South Coast Railway Company, series.

29. SS BRENTWOOD

The 1,179grt Cory-owned steam collier *Brentwood* had been built in 1904 to a size suited for Goole Docks. Such North-East coast ports supplied an ever increasing tonnage of coal to satisfy the demands of local gasworks (1800s onwards) and, electricity works (1900s on). *Brentwood* is seen in the c.1920 photograph berthed just upriver of Newhaven's swingbridge, at North Quay, discharging her inevitably dusty cargo by way of quayside steam cranes. A canvas has been draped across the bridge front to keep coal dust out of the accommodation. Astern of *Brentwood* lie a couple of elderly looking steam timber carriers, and a steam coaster is at the top end of the quay. In later years, Cory's adopted names all beginning with COR for their fleet - i.e. *Corwood*, etc.

30. SS DIEPPE

Built by Fairfields at Govan in 1905, *Dieppe* was Newhaven registered and of 1,426grt length 273ft breadth 35ft draught 14ft. She is the first turbine powered steamer to be mentioned in this book, and her engines could produce 6,500hp, giving a passage speed in excess of 21knots. She lasted until 1933 on the crossing. The postcard c.1922 shows her positively belting away from the berth, leaving anyone standing on the quayside coughing profusely from coal smoke! Note the rather unusual design of quayside cranes.

31. PORTSLADE GAS WORKS

Not quite in the seaside cheeky postcard idiom is this c.1905 view of Brighton & Hove Gas Company's Portslade Works. Presumably the Company could not resist the new medium of postcards to advertise their business. It is just as well that aromas are unprintable - the good folk of Portslade must have been delighted, on occasion, for the onslaught of a northerly breeze, to remind them of fresh air. Just discernible, lying at the wharf is one of Stephenson, Clarke's early steam colliers, possibly even *SS Portslade* with another 1,000 tons of gas making coal. This Company supplied coal until works closure. The Works opened in 1870 and by the time of closure c.1970 had seen various upgrades, and for a few latter years generation of gas from LPG.

32.1 SOUTHWICK LOCK

These two early postcards clearly show how little development had taken place along the old course of the Adur in the 50 years since the lock had been constructed in 1855. Both views are from c.1905. Lock dimensions were 175ft x 31ft. The view captures the early Brighton Corporation electricity generating station, which first produced power in 1897.

32.2

Below, the man perched on the lock gate balance arm is, like the old steamer, probably waiting for the tide for things to start happening. The area to the right of the lock was to see construction of the Prince George Lock in 1933 and the Prince Phillip Lock in 1957. The lock dimensions were 240ft x 40ft and 375ft x 57 ft.

33. SEASTONE

Dating from 1907 this humble workhorse of a vessel had an uncommonly long life and converted not only from steam to motor propulsion, but also in trade. Originally a Port of London Authority steam hopper dredger, later on named *James No.46*, she was converted in the early 1960s to a motor suction dredger, to win aggregates from the seabed. This metamorphosis also befell sister hopper *James No.47*. In the 1960s both ships, then renamed *Seastone* and *Rockstone* respectively, were often to be found along the Sussex Coast and Solent. The photograph taken in 1964 at Portslade Ballast Wharf shows *Seastone* in her Westminster Dredging Co. days, looking quite smart at 57 years. A modern wheelhouse, streamlined funnel and, of course, dredging gear, complete the conversion - the large crane is a quayside fixture. The wharf was sited right opposite the gasworks. *Seastone* and *Rockstone* survived another decade or so in the building trade boom times, being ultimately replaced by purpose built vessels.

34.1 LITTLEHAMPTON

Above, the ancient wooden chain ferry from Littlehampton to the Clymping shore is in mid-passage, bearing horse and cart c.1900. Just visible on the left is the bow of a sailing vessel moored at the railway wharf.

34.2

This view dates from 1908, and evidently heralds the grand opening of Littlehampton's first fixed link to the west bank, undoubtedly a red letter day. Rather a pleasing structure, with its operating cabin on high giving the 'bridgeman' ample warning of approaching river traffic, ready for opening. However, it had rather a narrow roadway and light load limit so by 1970 was somewhat outmoded. A modern structure subsequently was built some distance upstream, and a new retractable footbridge soon followed at this location. The old 1908 bridge was demolished in 1980.

34.3

This November 1908 dated photo captures the departure of Littlehampton's old chain ferry behind a steam tug. In the background, with opening day flags no longer flying, it's replacement sits astride the Arun, looking rather grand in comparison to a pontoon with hut. Moored nearby is a white hulled timber barquentine, seemingly all but ready for departure as she is riding high.

35. CLYMPING

A 'boomie' ketch of 121 tons, and another of the series constructed by Harvey's at their Clymping yard, Littlehampton, this example was built in 1909 and evidently from the sail patches, has been in trade for some time. In the photograph she appears to be setting off from Littlehampton in very light airs - the crew would seem to be watching the cameraman. Note the very slender topmast - the strain from the flying jib sail being taken partly by the stouter lower mast. A group of these old timers crossed the Atlantic c.1930 to continue trading in British Guiana, obsolete in their home waters. *Clymping*, *Kindly Light*, *Leading Light* and the Faversham schooner-barge *Goldfinch* undertook that great voyage.

36.1 ANNA

The 1909 built *Anna* was a steel hulled, Dutch vessel of 107 tons - a 'zeetjalk' - to accomplish similar trade functions to our own coastal sailing barges, they too had leeboards. Sometimes single masted, *Anna* was double or ketch in rig. Being auxiliary powered the type were particularly well suited to ports such as Rye where *Anna* used to bring a regular cargo of timber in the 1930s. The photograph shows her at the top end of Strand Quay lying ahead of a sailing barge. Note that Strand Quay had yet to be re-piled. A similar vessel *Katharina* was owned in Rye for some years around this time.

36.2 GWYNHELEN

The lower is a classic postcard view of Rye c.1930 and the sailing barge seen moored in the Brede cut is Samuel West's *Gwynhelen*, a 1909-built 71 tonner.

37.1 and 37.2

In this view of Rye from the South, one of the town's many sailing trawlers lies on the bed of the Rock Channel awaiting the tide. An indication of where *Gwynhelen* had been sitting is clear to see. This scene is probably pre-World War I. The second scene, with windmill and gas holder visible in the background, shows a small gaff cutter sitting on the slip while one of the boomie ketches lies further along Strand Quay and dates similarly.

38.1 SS ROUEN

The turbine powered *Rouen*, built in 1911, served the French Railway Company on the Newhaven-Dieppe route until the start of the World War II. She was of 1,656grt, measuring 292ft by 35ft beam. In the first war she had served the French Navy. The locally posted card (1924) shows her steaming into Newhaven on, judging by the flags, a special occasion - possibly the 1918 end of World War I. Note side decks had yet to evolve to fully covered in affairs.

38.2 Sheerlegs & WALBROOK

This 1964 photograph is of interest as Newhaven's well known landmark was only a year or so from demolition. Moored beneath them is the ex. Port of London Authority tug *Walbrook*, 168grt built in 1910. The Marine Workshops of the Railway Company visible in the background were still in full use, as indeed they had been since the 1880s.

39.1 SS SEABORNE ALPHA

This 1912 built 410grt steam coaster came from Rennoldson's yard at South Shields. She typifies the smaller size steamer of the day in coastal trades, and would originally have sported a single cargo derrick and steam winch. By the 1930s she was working for the Cement Marketing Company of London, and hence was probably well placed for conversion to a suction dredger, supplying sand and gravel to the building trade, a job she continued to do in the Solent and Sussex Coast areas right up to c. 1960. Remarkably little altered overall, the dredging pipe can be clearly seen, plus a small mast over the wheelhouse to hoist the dredging signal. The funnel emblem derives from her owners - Seaborne Aggregates.

39.2 SS MUNGRET

SS Mungret came from a Dublin Shipyard in 1912 and traded at first under the name *Sligo*. She operated in the general coasting trades for the Limerick Steam Ship Company. Of 515grt she makes an interesting comparison to *Seaborne Alpha*, with her bridge amidships instead of 'all-aft'. The ship has the traditional deep well deck forward of the bridge, however this feature is obscured by very high bulwarks. Seemingly, in this Littlehampton photograph, she has put her bow into a singularly inappropriate spot on the banks of the Arun, and is well aground awaiting the next high tide for refloating and escape to sea.

40. ST ADUR II

Built at South Shields in 1912, the 54 ton *Adur II* was of screw propulsion, unlike her predecessor at Shoreham Harbour. The 1930s postcard scene shows her heading out to sea with a pair of hopper barges astern, the 1933 lock gates not yet closed in the distance, behind the pole. This location as variously mentioned elsewhere is interesting for several reasons -

1. The Mystery/Nab Tower was built over to the right.
2. Kingston is where the River Adur finally settled its exit.
3. The chimneys of the 1906 electricity station are clearly visible.
4. The gasworks can just be made out behind the lockside flag pole.
5. The white cliffs beyond Brighton can be seen over the shingle bank.
6. Ladies' hats unmistakably 1930s.

Adur II had operated on the Portsmouth/Isle of Wight 'tow-boat' cargo service in her earlier years - the original pre-car ferry method of shifting cattle and vehicles across the Solent.

41. SS JB PADDON & STELLA →

With more demand for their seagoing coal scuttle brigade, Stephenson, Clarke added the *J.B.Paddon* to the fleet in 1917, along with the slightly smaller *SS Hove*. Both these ships came from the Scottish Company of G.Elsmie, Aberdeen. *Starbeam* became *J.B.Paddon*, and the *Collairnie, Hove*. For years thereafter, the 570grt. *J.B.Paddon* and 435grt *Hove* brought coal to Shoreham. The first named was sadly a Second World War loss; whereas *Hove* had gone to Coppack Brothers in 1935 and traded until demolition at Dublin in 1961. The photograph taken at Southwick old lock is pretty much the reverse view of the *Adur II* scene. On this occasion the old paddle tug *Stella* would seem to be out of commission, c.1920.

42. SS AGHIOS GIORGIOS II →

Bergen built and owned in Norway, this 1916 constructed steamer had originally been named *Snar*, then *Finse*. Of 1,653grt 2,385dwt she had been updated with oil firing, but like many veteran steamers of the type, could no longer compete with modern motor tonnage. *Finse* went to Eastern Mediterranean owners who, no doubt, had hoped to get a few more years out of the old ship. In 1963, now in Lebanese hands, she was proceeding up the English Channel with a full cargo of esparto grass (used in paper manufacture) when fire caught hold, in mid-channel. The fire raged for days and the ship was ultimately beached at Norman's Bay, east of Eastbourne. It was often said that esparto grass, carried in loosely compressed bales, could spontaneously combust. However, it spread throughout the old steamer, leaving this sad and much heat twisted wreck to be later removed and duly scrapped at 47 years of age. Another unwarranted but brief tourist attraction in East Sussex. When merely about one year into service, as *Snar*, the ship had spent two weeks aground close to St.Catherine's Point, on the Isle of Wight, during World War I. She was lightened, towed off and repaired at Southampton in November 1917.

43. REINA II

A 1930's view at the Aldrington end of Southwick Canal shows an interesting auxiliary powered schooner of Dutch origin. It would appear to be about to load scrap. Craft of this type were common around the North European coasts from c.1910, this example started out as a lofty twin masted schooner, with long bowsprit. Steel hulls predominated in Holland's shipbuilding long before British or Scandinavian coasters gave up wooden hulls. In the search for efficiencies of operation, *Reina II* has lost her topmasts, had half the bowsprit removed and lost the mizzen gaff and boom. It also had fitted an engine exhaust pipe, only just short of a funnel, to clear the motor fumes away. Many examples of these attractive little ships then lasted in trade right up to the 1960's, as fully powered motorships. This one has retained a foresail and mainsail, for favourable conditions. Some had many owners over the years and indeed if a reader can confirm the ship's original name, the author would be delighted to hear.

44. MOULTONIAN

The last wooden coastal trading ketch built at the Clymping Yard of Harvey's, Littlehampton, and the last in Sussex, *Moultonian* drew wooden commercial cargo ship construction to an end in the county. At 164grt and 240dwt tons, the 100ft by 23ft vessel with a draught of 8.5ft, entered service ketch rigged. Registered at Littlehampton throughout her long career, the ship received her first auxiliary oil engines in 1928. In the 1930s she was trading for Thomas Price of Newport, I.O.W., and again received new engines in 1940. This time a pair of Bergius oil engines, driving the twin screws. Later she came under Vectis Shipping's fleet, continuing in trade until dismantled at the end of the 1960s, at Southampton. The 1930s photograph shows the ship still with main and after mast, but no longer rigged to carry sail. She is sharing a dock at Southampton with a steam tug and one of the Railway Company's cross Channel cargo steamers. The massive London and South Western Railway Company warehouse c.1897 is much evident. *Moultonian's* immediate predecessor, *Wessex* of 1918, 148grt also had a very similar career. Owned in the 1930s by Charles Price of Newport, and later Williams Shipping of Southampton, she traded until c.1955. *Moultonian* dates from 1919.

45.1 Scandinavian timber ships at Littlehampton

An unidentified barquentine of probably Danish origin is seen here reducing canvas as she is entering Littlehampton Harbour. Craft of this type were regular traders with Baltic timber in the season, right up to WWII. From the elevated position of a crewman, she is evidently carrying a good deck load of timber. Wooden hulled traders of this type were often auxiliary motor fitted, and some survived into the 1950s.

45.2 FLORA

The second ship is of different rig, being a three masted schooner with a square topsail. *Flora*, 306 tons, built in 1919, has just left her berth, having discharged, and judging by the lighthouse windvane has a light north-westerly for the start of her voyage. A sizeable crowd have gathered as ever on the pier to witness the departure - at least one having arrived by motor bike. These vessels were amongst the last true sailing types to regularly appear in the Sussex ports.

45.3 CHRISTENSEN

Towing to sea in c.1920 is another Scandinavian timberman, the *Christensen*. This vessel looks immaculately kept with no patches in the sails and may indeed have been a new ship at the time. Swedish and Danish builders were still turning out cargo sailing ships with wooden hulls in 1920, and indeed up to WWII. Most became auxiliary motor powered and many traded on until the 1960s.

46. Steam Coaster entering Littlehampton

A small steam coaster enters the River Arun on a fine, calm day and is evidently letting 'rip' on her whistle, perhaps to give fair warning to the swing bridge operator to do his stuff. Although again unidentified, this little steamer, of the bridge amidships type, would have been one amongst hundreds similar. From her trim she would appear to be entering Littlehampton to load. Approx. tonnage 400grt, and year of build around 1919. Again the photograph is c.1930s.

47. SS REX

Rex visited the River Adur at Shoreham in 1961 with timber from the Baltic. Built in 1919 at Moss, Norway, the triple expansion steam engined ship is an excellent example of the 'Baltic' type timber carrier, although she would carry any dry cargo on offer. Masts and derrick posts are sited each end of the hatch areas, steam winches are raised, and the derricks, shown stowed, would lay on top of any timber deck cargo, so carried. *Rex* was of 1,182grt, 1,800dwt, and could probably manage about 9-10 knots - fast enough at the time for the timber trade. In the photograph c.1950s, the old ship is looking particularly well cared for, considering her 40 years. She traded on into the 60s for her owner, O.Torgersen, of Haugesund, Norway.

48. Sunset over Aldrington Basin

This is a particularly unusual postcard and a little difficult to accurately date. Two differing design steam coasters lie alongside, one of the old open-bridge type, the other shows the trend with a properly closed-in wheelhouse, and, less commonly for the period, a grey hull. Beyond, at least two sailing ships are moored, judging by the forest of masts, in line. Flags appear to denote some special occasion - could it be the end of the First World War? In the foreground some work appears to be underway on the old sluice through to the, as yet, undeveloped Hove Lagoon marsh. Can anyone identify these steamers, etc?

49. The Mystery Tower

Amidst great secrecy during the latter stages of World War I, the local population witnessed the skyward construction of two of these massive concrete and steel towers. The discussion surrounding their ultimate use and destination was no doubt rife, but the war had ended before their completion. It is likely that they were intended for the narrow part of the Dover Strait, where shipping movements could be controlled by anti-submarine nets. The tower nearest completion was finished off in 1920 and taken away by Admiralty tugs, to replace the Nab Shoal Lightship, a few miles south-east of the Isle of Wight. Once settled on the seabed and with a slight lean, it still provides the Nab Tower light, and barring any further advances from wayward banana carriers, may it long continue so to do. The least completed tower was cleared from the Shoreham Harbour building site by 1924, by dismantling.

50. SS JELLICOE ROSE

Not exactly a high scorer in the beauty stakes, the 1920 built *Jellicoe Rose* was nevertheless an efficient steam coaster. This layout was not so common with two hatches forward and one abaft the bridge. The three derrick masts giving the old ship almost a schooner appearance. A product of Burntisland shipyard in Scotland, at 220ft by 34ft with a draught of 13ft, she was suited to the new 1933 lock at Southwick. Tonnages were 1,118 gross and 1,550 deadwt. The photograph shows her leaving Shoreham probably for the next cargo of coal. She served owners Hughes, Holden of Liverpool for decades in the coasting trade, along with some similar sized sister vessels. In 1956 she went 'foreign' and carried on a bit longer under the Panamanian flag as *Conchita*.

51. SS DONA FLORA

Dona Flora, at 786grt came from Haverton Hill on Tees in 1924, and was also owned locally at Middlesbrough by T.H.Donking & Sons; Kingdon Steamship Co. A sister ship was *Dona Isabel*. The ships were general traders of the day, but coal cargoes were probably frequent. The ship presents another slight design variation for coasters, the mainmast is just ahead of the after block, instead of the rear of the bridge structure. Like many coasters, a semi-permanent long ladder is lashed up the rigging for shore access in berths where the tide has gone out, or similar local difficulties arise. In the mid 1950s *Dona Flora* went to the Holderness SS Co. who specialised in old steamers, when others were giving up. Briefly, she traded as *Holdernett*. In the photograph she is just entering between the old wooden breakwaters at Shoreham.

← 52. ST FOREMOST 22

The 1924 steam tug *Foremost 22* was built at Zaltbommel in the Netherlands. Of 211grt her 650 hp, steam engine was both large and powerful enough for local duties at Newhaven, and salvage in the English Channel, should the occasion require. She was also fitted for fire fighting. Actually ordered by the London, Brighton and South Coast Railway Company, she entered service with the Southern Railway, and saw service too with British Railways until sale in 1960. After another 18 years service with Italian owners, the old tug was broken up in Italy in 1978.

53. WILL EVERARD

Although steel hulled and built as late as 1925, this coastal auxiliary sailing barge has the appearance and layout of earlier examples. A quartet of these proportions came from the Great Yarmouth yard of Fellowes, and great load carriers they were. At 188grt and 280dwt and manageable by two or three crew, this was more or less the pinnacle size-wise for barges. The 1950s photograph shows the *Will Everard* motoring whilst mainsail and top might be giving help in the light airs. The mizzen sail is brailed into the mast and no fore sails are set the bowsprit being raised. This barge, last of her quartet, still visited Newhaven to load cement on occasions, or to seek shelter from Channel gales right into the 1960s. Latterly, the bowsprit and mizzen mast were completely removed. Owners F.T.Everard & Son had the traditional barge scroll work painted in gold at bow and stern rail boards. Later, Will Everard dropped the 'Everard' part of the name as she became a kind of 'corporate entertainment centre' within the P&O. Group. This saw her fully restored and very active again.

54. SS PASS OF MELFORT

By the standards of her year of construction, the steam coastal tanker *Pass of Melfort* was quite large and advanced in design. From Blythswood Shipbuilding in Glasgow in 1926, she could carry about 750tons of clean petroleum products to coastal installations from the refineries, for her owners, Bulk Oil Steam Ship Company. The Company ran a fleet of about half a dozen similar size ships eventually being absorbed into the Cory Group. The unusual purple banded, white ringed funnel being replaced by their familiar white band and black diamond. Note the spark arrester on the funnel and cargo pumproom top on the tanktop, with vents in the customary one on and one off the wind manner, for its ventilation. Ships of this type were becoming more frequent visitors to ports like Shoreham in the 1930s, as motor transport grew. Later, industry started converting wholesale to oil firing of boilers, so the tanker fleet mushroomed, especially after World War II.

A new motor tanker of the same name, but 970 tons, appeared in 1961.

55. MT CALDERGATE

The Anglo American Oil Company had this sturdy little motor tanker built at Amble in 1927. Her dimensions were very modest: length 97ft breadth 17ft with an 8ft 5ins draught. However the layout was classic and with motor propulsion, an evolutionary step had transpired. In subsequent decades the Company became 'ESSO', or Eastern States Standard Oil, and the little *Caldergate* continued to be active right up to the 1960s, mostly on estuarial duties. Note this is the first fully powered motor ship to appear in this book.

56. PS SUSSEX QUEEN

A product of Samuel White's Shipyard at Cowes, Isle of Wight this attractive little steamer was built for the Southern Railway's Lymington to Yarmouth Pier passenger service in 1927. Named *Freshwater* she continued in that employment for quite some time even after the introduction of the first car carriers to the route in 1938. By the 1950s she was kept as a relief vessel for the busy summer traffic, however by the end of the 1950s was surplus to requirements. Of 264grt, and a mere 159ft in length by 43ft over the paddleboxes, she drew only 5ft 7ins of water, constrained by the shallow Lymington River. In 1960 a brief period operating excursions along the Sussex Coast ensued, as *Sussex Queen*. Finishing her days as *Swanage Queen* c.1961, the scrapyard took her despite a valiant last attempt at preservation. The photograph shows *Sussex Queen* little altered from her railway days, except for the provision of a mainmast, to support a second steaming light as then required by new Collision Regs. A good crowd appear to be enjoying a lumpy sea trip, one hopes. In earlier years as *Freshwater* a steadying 'staysail' was sometimes hoisted on the forestay, to help turn the vessel in the Lymington River. An unusual feature, also found in her predecessors, was a small wheelhouse but no bridge structure.

← 57. MV FERROCRETE

Faversham built at Pollock's yard in 1927, the 158grt, 100ft long *Ferrocrete* belonged to the Associated Portland Cement Marketing Company of London. In the decades leading up to the closure of Asham Cement Works on the River Ouse between Newhaven and Lewes, this smart little motor coaster joined the older *Celtic* in transporting cement to the Isle of Wight, carrying just under 200 tons per trip. This was a good sized cargo for a ship drawing a mere 7ft 6in, admirable for both the River Ouse in Sussex and River Medina on the Isle of Wight, where similar tight constraints applied. In the photograph c.1950s, *Ferrocrete* is winding her way down to the sea at Newhaven. The cement works lies behind the mast.

← 58. SS WORTHING

Denny of Dumbarton produced some of the most attractive, well balanced design ferries, ever seen on cross-channel routes These craft seemed to have almost a 'family' likeness to each other, and this was particularly true for the Southern Railway's ships. Dating from 1928, the steam turbine powered *Worthing* was a fine example at 304ft in length and 2,294grt. She could maintain a speed of 25 kts on the Newhaven to Dieppe route. After a career of 27 years, finishing with British Railways, she went out to Greece in 1955 for further service with Latsis Lines, as *Phyrni*, finally reaching the scrapyard in 1964. The early 1950s photograph shows her well laden with passengers slicing across the Channel at full tilt, the fine lines of the hull much in evidence. Note also, compared to earlier ships featured on the route, the closing in of side alleyways this giving much more accommodation space for inclement weather.

59. MV ANNA

Pre World War II, and again up to the 1960s before Rye Harbour Wharf was constructed, Dutch motor coasters would bring Baltic timber cargoes up the River Tillingham to Rye's Strand quay. Usually these cargoes were of about 200 tons, or 60-70 standards of timber. Larger than the 1909 *Anna*, the zeetjalk already described, the 1929 *Anna* was of 190grt and had started out as *Arma*, being built in the Dutch town of Groningen, as a fully powered motorship. She, in common with many of her contemporaries, probably carried some sail to aid the voyage on occasion in her earlier years. The aerial photograph is a delight as it not only typifies the kind of craft that used to come up to Strand Quay, but represents a way of life now vanished. The photo dates from the early 1950s. Often with these little ships the Master was the owner as well, and possibly the crew were his sons and or brothers. Frequently, wife and whole family lived aboard. In the picture, *Anna* is awaiting tide and Pilot, and judging by the laundry drying in the breeze on the poop deck they are perhaps all hoping for a run ashore. The well stowed timber cargo extends right onto the forecastle head, and still the little ship is only just down to her marks.

60. Ford Railway Bridge, River Arun

Sometimes referred to as a swingbridge, this structure was in fact, nothing of the kind. It was a side sliding drawbridge and with the aid of an eight to ten man gang, could be lifted slightly, and then drawn onto the western side, over the fixed track, in the Ford direction. The time taken to disconnect rails and signal wires, to let a ship pass through, then return to status quo was reportedly only thirty minutes, or thereabouts. Railway records state that in any case between 1919 and 1928, "the bridge had not to be opened for masted vessels", Arundel's trade already having gone to Littlehampton. The man leaning on the boardwalk in this 1929 photograph may have a very long wait to see a ship pass through the 40 ft wide navigable channel, the final bridge opening was in 1936. With impending electrification of the line and trains having become heavier over the years, the Southern Railway put a fixed replacement bridge in place ready for 1938.

61.1 SS LA PLATA →

Danish built at Nakskov in 1930, this 1,600grt steamer had acquired its sixth name by 1964 when the photo was taken. *La Plata* was Uruguayan owned and Panamanian flagged, and is seen discharging South American timber at Shoreham. Oil fired boilers provided steam for a quadruple expansion engine - these becoming more popular at the time of her construction.

61.2 SS VARD ↘

A good example of the larger 'Baltic' type of timberman is the Norweigian owned and registered *Vard*, built also in 1930 but only on her second name here in 1963, at Shoreham. At 3,150dwt she belonged with a couple of similar vessels to Egil Naesheim, and was much into the White Sea timber trade, from Russia. The 900 standards of timber would very likely have at least in part been stowed by Russian women stevedores. These cargoes were very labour intensive taking many days to strop ashore even with large gangs. *Vard* too, was powered by a quadruple expansion steam engine, and she soldiered on to complete forty years service.

62. MV MEDINA

This is the second vessel in this book to have started life as a member of Red Funnel Steamers Isle of Wight service, in whose employ she was the first motor ferry. Only 143ft in length by 28ft beam she was functional rather than attractive in design. At the after end there was a small car deck - shades of many things to come - twin Gardner diesels and propellers did not give her much speed. For their next vessel Red Funnel reverted to another paddle steamer. In 1962 with larger purpose built car ferries arriving on the route, *Medina* went out to Gibraltar for further service, but later returned to the UK for use in static roles, such as this clubhouse at the then new Brighton Marina, c.1978. *Medina* came from Thornycroft's Southampton yard in 1931. Note the upper deck has been boxed in for the clubhouse role.

63. MT TILLERMAN

C.Rowbotham's 220grt motor tanker was also the shape of things to come when she appeared in 1931 from the De Noord shipyard in the Netherlands. Capable of visiting the smallest coastal oil depots she did just that until the early 1960s, when replaced by an 800 tonner of the same name. Rowbothams were a very old company having started with steam coasters. Oil products were at first carried in 'cases' by the traditional cargo vessels of the day, demand being low. The fleet of specialised motor tankers grew from the 1930s, and they will feature again later in the book. The Company has seen some mixed fortunes over the years with one or two parent company changes. Several members of the fleet regularly visited Shoreham installations for many years.

64. SS FOREMOST PRINCE

The James Dredging, Towage and Transport Company were much involved with harbour dredging services. Their 1933 built, 849grt steam bucket dredger came from Blythswood, Glasgow, and is seen at work in the approaches to Newhaven Harbour. By manoeuvring herself on mooring wires by steam winches, the channel will be cleared and the deposits 'shuted' into barges alongside for towage to the dumping grounds, well offshore. Such was the importance placed in keeping the fairways open at all states of the tide for the railway ferries, that another dredger, the smaller *Testside*, was also employed at Newhaven. *Foremost Prince*, less commonly for the type, had a proper bridge right forward and her own steam engine being able to undertake voyages to wherever the next job loomed.

65.1 SS PETWORTH

At 977grt, 1,465dwt the 1934 built *Petworth* illustrates the ever growing size of steam colliers, to satisfy the gas and electricity generation demands. It will be seen that no cargo gear was fitted to the majority of these vessels, being reliant on shore gear for loading and at the other end for discharge. By 1957, once colliers of 3-4,000 tons could enter Shoreham, the *Petworth* was sold to Onesimus Dorey of Guernsey, and she gave them another three years service before scrapping in Holland under her new name of *Belvedere*. The photograph shows her steaming out of Shoreham Harbour in the early 1950s, two crewmen securing the anchors and putting away the ropes, ready for the passage north-east, and more coal.

65.2 SS OLAV ASBJØRN

Registered in Copenhagen to Olav Line, the 1934 built *Olav Asbjørn* represents a typical general cargo carrier of the period, with bridge amidships, and a full set of cargo derricks, arranged in pairs for 'union-purchase' operation. As seen at Shoreham, shore craneage had taken over, with rolls of newsprint off-loading. *Olav Asbjørn* had a set of quadruple expansion steam engines plus a refinement in the form of a low pressure steam turbine. This ship was of 1,612grt.

66. MT BEN OLIVER

Rowhedge Ironworks, Colchester built this sturdy little motor tanker in 1935 for National Benzole. She could carry about 140 tons of petroleum products - something equivalent to five modern articulated truck loads, in today's terms. At 95ft by 19ft, *Ben Oliver* was the smallest in her owners coastal fleet. Not long after this 1950s photograph was taken, the half dozen vessels were merged into the Shell-Mex/BP integrated operation. The familiar National Benzole motif on the funnel being replaced by a yellow band between two white rings, on a black funnel. In the 1960s outsized by newer ships, *Ben Oliver* went to work as a sand suction dredger, in the Solent area.

67. SS LECONFIELD

Once Littlehampton's grab dredger, the 91grt steamer *Leconfield* came from Philips Shipyard, Dartmouth. She put in 25 years work at Littlehampton, before moving west to the Solent for further employment. She was smartly kept, but when this 1973 photo was taken at Newport, I.O.W. the old ship was awaiting the scrapman's torch. In earlier days, a Priestman steam crane would have been fitted to grab the harbour mud and drop it into the hopper. *Leconfield* was built in 1935.

68. MV SAND MARTIN

A very familiar sight along the Sussex Coast in the 1950s and 1960s, this 633grt sand suction dredger was, at the time, the largest in her owner South Coast's fleet. Built as a cargo ship named *Rookwood*, she was a very early convert to the building trade supply fleet, this happened in 1940, only six years after her construction. Newer purpose-built vessels having arrived, the old *Sand Martin* finally went to Irish breakers at Cork in 1974.

69. SS ARTHUR WRIGHT

In pre-nationalisation days, the electricity generating companies were many and diverse. Brighton Corporation, one of the most progressive, took delivery of two new steam colliers to serve their 1906 plant on Southwick Canal. Built by North Eastern Marine, Sunderland, the 1,091grt *Arthur Wright* and running mate *Henry Moon* (a war loss), were well suited to the new lock at Southwick. (Prince George, 1933). Unusually for steam colliers these two ships had grey hulls, and blue, black topped funnels with the black motif letters EBU on a white band. This indicated 'Brighton Electricity Undertaking'. In 1948 the surviving steamer went into the British Electricity Authority fleet. Livery: black hull, red funnel, two black rings and black top together with the white letters B.E.A. The photograph is from the 1948-54 period, after which the letters became C.E.A. In 1958 the letters were abandoned altogether. Noteworthy in the picture is the radar installation upgrade also a new lightweight signal mast for the regulatory extra steaming light. In 1957, surplus to requirements, *Arthur Wright* went to the Swedish Flag as *Ariston*, serving until scrapping in Denmark in 1963. A reasonable length career from 1937.

70. PS RYDE

In quieter winter periods the Portsmouth-Ryde paddlers were often to be found at Newhaven, undergoing repair, survey and a lick of paint in readiness for the busy season. This state of affairs had existed from London Brighton & South Coast Railway days, through Southern Railway, and British Railways, right up to British Rail's days. *Ryde*, another Denny of Dumbarton product, served the Isle of Wight from 1937 until 1967, the last paddler on the route. She survived just long enough to be adorned with British Rail's two-way-arrow sign, on the funnel, plus the blue and grey livery. On retirement, a sort of static career ensued as a nightclub on the River Medina, near Newport, IOW. Some time later, fire and dereliction took over. In the 1993 photograph she still appears reasonably intact - looks can be deceptive, and what a great shame that preservation evaded her - as her neighbour at this location, the *Medway Queen* now back in Kent is at least on the road to recovery in preservation hands. *Ryde*, 566grt, was the last of the Portsmouth paddlers, the *Sandown* having gone to scrap just a couple of years earlier.

71. MV DRAKE →

The General Steam Navigation Company of London had a very large fleet engaged in general cargo liner services around North West Europe and to the Mediterranean. Their ships were always smartly kept, and had a distinguishing white line along the topsides. Built at Groningen, Holland, the 531grt *Drake*, although of the traditional midships design, was, in 1937, progressive with motor propulsion. She has single derricks to serve the one long and one shorter after hold, presenting an attractive workmanlike appearance. One of the Company trades was to French Bay of Biscay ports and it was in that capacity that the ship visited Shoreham's Aldrington Basin, where the Company had a terminal up to the 1960s. In the photograph *Drake* looks to be fresh from drydock, and the pilot ladder hangs in readiness over the side. In common with many ships in the 1950s, radar had yet to be fitted.

72. TSS EMPRESS QUEEN

In the late 1930s, P.& A. Campbell decided to build a large, fast steamer for the long distance excursion trade, and this was at the time an idea bordering on 'rocket technology' compared to their steam paddler fleet. An order was placed with Ailsa of Troon, Scotland for a steam turbine powered steamer capable of 18 knots, and indeed when launched in 1940, the result was almost of cross-channel proportions, and a very attractive ship indeed. War, of course, intervened and the 1,760grt *Empress Queen* went straight into Navy service. Not a good start. The ship's engines consisted of four sets of steam turbines built by Harland and Wolff. On subsequent entry into commercial service after a post war refit, it seems that events conspired against the ship - the old pre-war devoted trippers did not return in any great numbers, the ship proving difficult to fill and costly to run. The great British public were beginning to discover other pastimes, and by 1951 *Empress Queen* went to Greece as *Philippos*, never having reached her potential in home waters.

73. SS ESSO TIOGA

An occasional visitor to Esso's small terminal at Aldrington Basin, this rather plain looking tanker started out as one of a large series of war built standard types. Several classes, both steam and motor powered appeared from various yards, basic but robust. After the war many survivors joined the major oil fleets, and then gave many years of good service, up to the 1960s. *Esso Tioga*, 797grt, ex *Empire Wrestler*, was triple expansion powered, and could manage about 9kts. In the 1950s photograph she is gas freeing the tanks with the traditional method of canvas wind-sail vents, hanging from the stay. Very efficient they were, too, and with a long canvas tail could direct the breeze right to the bottom of the tanks.

74. MV PEN ADUR

In 1961 two small cargo vessels arrived on the Sussex Coast for conversion to sand suction dredgers. These were the *Lerryn* and the *Lantyan*, both 300 tons, and of another wartime standard type from 1943. After conversion for their new trade by Taylors Shipyard on Shoreham Beach, they were then constantly running for several years to Sussex ports, from the Channel dredging grounds. Lerryn was renamed *Pen Adur*, Lantyan becoming *Pen Arun*, and the first ship later served as *Sand Wren*. In this 1970 Littlehampton photograph, *Pen Adur* has discharged her cargo at owner's Penfolds wharf, and awaits the tide to get away for the next load. In the distance, beyond the 1908 swingbridge can just be made out the bow of *Suavity*.

75.1 MV SAND SKIPPER

Once the *Empire Skipper*, and generally similar to the *Pen Adur*, this little ship was a much earlier convert to the ballast trade. In 1947, the *Skipper* and an identical sister vessel *Sand Runner*, started running along the South Coast. The ships were built in 1943. The aerial photograph c.1950s, shows the ship in action on the dredging ground, with suction pipe lowered on the starboard side, and the sandy/watery mix gradually filling the single hold. Special large drainage scupper pipes drain excess water overboard. A kind of chute is rigged to lead the sand to the corners of the hold for an even stow. On arrival in port, shore grab crane discharge was the only option.

75.2 MT OCEAN PULLER

Handling a hopper barge at Newhaven in 1978 is *Ocean Puller*, 1943 built, 145grt.

76. ST CHRIANIE

In the 1960s a decision was taken to replace the Royal Sovereign Lightship with a fixed light tower and accommodation module. The firm engaged to carry out this work was Christiani and Neilsen, who then utilised an area just east of Newhaven Harbour for construction and preparation of the separate tower and module, before it was taken the few miles south east of Beachy Head - its final home. To service the site, the ex navy tug T.I.D.107, named *Chrianie*, was based at Newhaven for some time. She was one of over a hundred identical standard wartime built tugs the T.I.D. standing in naval parlance for Tug, Inshore Duties. These little steam tugs, built in 1944, were just basic harbour duty craft. However after the war, the majority of survivors went into civilian ownership. Newhaven had already seen many years good service from *Tidworth*, another of the series. In the photograph c.1967 at Newhaven, *Chrianie* awaits action, on one of the stages, and across the river, so does *PS Ryde*, and the *Maid of Orleans*, too, await the summer season.

77.1 SS LEVENWOOD

Constantine Lines of Middlesbrough, an old established company, ran steam and motor coasters, plus ocean ships. The 1945 *Levenwood* at 1,058grt represents another war time standard design, this being a handy size steam coaster. She was built at Greenock under the name *Empire Bromley*. In the 1950s photo she is about to lock-out at Southwick.

77.2 SS BP MANAGER

The 1945 steam tanker *Empire Tesland*, joined the Shell BP fleet after the war, and was jumboised with an extra 40ft hull section, thereby increasing her gross tonnage from 979 to 1,149. In the photograph c.1950s the extra bit is noticeable - between midships and aft appears elongated. *BP Manager* used to call at Portslade.

78. SS OLIVER BURY

Just before the nationalisation of the regional electricity producers, the London Power Company ordered this 4,310dwt ton steam collier from Hall Russell, Aberdeen. In 1948 she went to the nationalised British Electricity Authority fleet. Towards the end of her coal carrying career the old ship on occasion, visited Shoreham after 1957, and on spring tides. The photograph in 1970 shows her turning ready for the berth and the power station grabs, just before her sale to Cypriot owners, for whom she gave a couple of years service. As *Alycia* she went to La Spezia scrapyard in 1973. Note - the small but traditionally wood faced wheelhouse - not a feature much seen later than her 1946 date of build.

79.1 and 79.2 SS KEYNES

A regular weekly visitor to Newhaven for twenty years, usually bringing coal from Seaham Harbour, for the various town gasworks around East Sussex, this 1,563grt steamer was built in 1946. *Keynes* was of the old triple expansion engine type and came out of North Eastern Marine's Shipyard at Sunderland. The second ship of this name in Stephenson Clarke's fleet, at 270ft by 37ft, with a draught just under 17ft, she was about the maximum size to percolate through Newhaven's ancient swingbridge, the weekly 2,000 tons of gas making coal being unloaded at the top end of North Quay. By 1967 *Keynes* was made redundant by extending gas mains from Portslade into East Sussex. She went to Swedish owners, but after a mere three years, was scrapped at Gothenburg as *Granita IV*.

80. SS LONDONBROOK

A steam coaster very much of pre-war layout, *Londonbrook* came from the shipyard of J. Lewis at Aberdeen in 1946. At 946grt, she was one of a quartet of sister ships employed in the coastal trades by Comben, Longstaff and Co who ran a fleet of a dozen or so. By the mid fifties motor ships gradually replaced the old steamers. In the photograph c.1962 at North Quay, Newhaven, Londonbrook awaits the tide - 15ft 3in on the draught stick over the stern, means not enough water to go anywhere, just yet. *Londonbrook* was radar fitted and the cook is stoking up the galley range.

81. MV SUAVITY →

F.T.Everard & Sons recognised the cost savings and efficiencies achieved by motor ships very early in the 20th century. Their *Suavity*, 943grt, built at Grangemouth in 1946 and one of many similar, makes an interesting comparison to *Londonbrook*, virtually the same size and intended employment. She was fitted with derricks for general trading. If *Suavity's* funnel were taller, she would still have passed as a steam coaster in layout. In the 1970 photograph at Littlehampton's Railway Quay, indeed, railway wagons are still in use on the craned quayside. Before many more years passed, all four Sussex ports lost the rail connection, - in the name of progress.

82. SS ALEXANDROS X

When photographed in 1968 at Southwick Canal Turning Basin, this Greek flagged general cargo steamer would have seen a few names and owners. At 2,106grt, the 1946 built ship would be increasingly expensive both to man and maintain, and even to fuel. The timber trade from the Black Sea would be a likely area of operation. Moored in a lay-by berth, no doubt the crew are hoping for some voyage orders, soon. Ships of this size could only reach this location post the 1957 harbour redevelopments at Shoreham.

← 84. MV RENNES

In 1947, French Railways introduced new motor cargo ships to the Newhaven - Dieppe route, replacing elderly steamers. The 1,053grt *Rennes* and sister vessels *Nantes* and *Brest* ran on services parallel to the passenger vessels, and would carry anything on offer. All cargo had of course to be craned on and off these hard working craft. The 1963 photograph shows *Rennes* entering Newhaven, and careful examination of the maindeck reveals two or three cars, plus a pair of the early small road/rail containers, that had been in use for some years. As *Rennes* appears quite deeply loaded, there must be a fair tonnage of general goods, down in the hold. This kind of operation was largely abandoned within a very few years, as the Ro-Ro's swiftly mopped up the traffic; now trucks motored directly into and indeed through Europe.

← 83. PS WAVERLEY

Clyde built by A.& J.Inglis in 1947, for River Clyde services, *Waverley* is indeed the last sea-going paddler. At 693grt, 240ft in length by 58ft over the paddle boxes, she is powered by a three crank triple expansion engine, and economically runs at about 14 knots. In 1975 the operation of the ship passed to the PSPS (Paddle Steamer Preservation Society), and gradually she operated further afield from her home waters. This gave the opportunity for paddle steamer trips in areas long bereft of their own paddlers. Regular overhauls and major upgrades keep the old ship in tiptop condition, largely by volunteer work, so she should be able to continue for years to come. In the 1978 photograph, *Waverley* has just set off from Worthing Pier for an evening 'one way trip' back to the Solent. Sadly, by the end of the 20th century, rather fewer piers are still fit and able to receive the ship's periodic visitations.

85. SS FALAISE

Another Denny of Dumbarton build, this passenger ferry clearly indicates the increase in ship size on the Newhaven/Dieppe route. A turbine powered steamer of 3,710grt *Falaise* was selected to be converted in 1963 to drive-on/drive-off or roll-on/roll-off mode to relaunch the Dieppe service. This sadly sounded the death knell for other ships on two counts namely, passengers took to their cars, and freight took to the new system with great haste. The 25 knot dashes of traditional passenger ferries soon came to an end, as fewer rail passengers appeared for the conventional rail connection system. It must be said that the stern appearance of *Falaise* (photo 68) was not greatly enhanced by the new door. This form of modificaton did however give several railway steamers, whose dimensions permitted, a new lease of life, as Ro-Ro *Falaise* went to scrap in 1974, a good length career from 1947.

86.1 SS BRANKSOME

This 1,438grt steam collier was of the old order, triple expansion powered giving about 10 knots speed, she could carry a little under 2000 tons of coal. After a career of only 14 years in the coal trade, she went foreign in 1962, lasting only until 1969 before scrapping in Bilbao, Spain. A very short career for a ship built in 1948.

86.2 MV BROADHURST

Also built in 1948 *Broadhurst* was a motorship of 1,171grt and shows the way forward in collier evolution. Both these ships had mechanical hatch covers - the various forms of winch pulled wires being clearly visible. Even for the more efficient motor ship, the fact that the coal trade was declining saw the Broadhurst broken up at Blyth in 1968, a few months before *Branksome*.

87. SS LUGANO

Larger steam colliers were still being built in 1949, when the Hudson Steamship Company ordered several. This example had spent about twenty years as *Hudson Firth* and, although basically built to large collier dimensions, she was fitted at the outset with a full set of derricks and cargo gear. This would enable the ship to trade outside Europe and, indeed, *Hudson Firth* sometimes brought sugar back from the West Indies in her earlier years. Photographed in Shoreham's Eastern Arm 1970, the ship had left the British Flag, passing to Greek owners and Panamanian flag. A very large timber cargo discharge has just got underway. Built at Troon, Scotland by Ailsa Shipbuilders, most unusually the old steamer went to breakers at Dalmuir, in 1973. Gross tonnage, 3,117.

88.1 MV COMITY

Looking very ship-shape on a ballast voyage for the next cargo is the 1949 built 198grt *Comity*, of F.T.Everard & Sons, Ltd. This little motor coaster would on occasion stand in on the Asham cement trade, when others needed drydocking.

88.2 MV AGNES

Another 1949 built ship, the Dutch *Agnes*, 386grt is seen in this 1970s photograph passing Rye Harbour village on her way up the River Rother to the loading berth. Pre war the Dutch coaster fleet was composed of many 200 ton ships. *Agnes* could probably lift about 400, and would appear to be about to do so, at Rye.

89.1 SS MAID OF ORLEANS

The 1949, Denny built *Maid* was generally in service on the Dover Strait routes for British Railways, however this 1965 photograph sees her in Newhaven for attention at the Marine Workshops. Similarly just astern, *PS Ryde* also in the new livery - quite revolutionary then. *Maid of Orleans* was 3,777grt 341ft by 52ft and 12ft draught.

89.2
SS BRIGHTON

The 1950 built *Brighton*, was the last conventional passenger ship that Denny's completed for the Dieppe route. At 2,875grt 312ft by 43ft and 11ft draught, two steam turbines gave the ship a speed of 24kts. In the 1963 photograph, the ship is arriving at Newhaven. *Brighton* was not a convert for Ro-Ro operations, being sold a few years later.

90. SS CLIFF QUAY

Six vessels of this 4,600dwt size were built c.1950 to serve Thames side plus Ipswich power stations. *Cliff Quay*, named after the latter's power station and the first to be built, became the last survivor of the group. Pickersgill built at Sunderland, these ships were 339ft long 46ft beam and 20ft draught. The 1957 lock at Southwick and redevelopments at Shoreham enabled the larger colliers to visit the power station, especially on Spring tides. The Autumn 1983 photograph has significance as this was the very end of 150 years of steam colliers around the United Kingdom coasts. Astern of *Cliff Quay* lies the new motor collier *Kindrence* described later in the book. *Cliff Quay* went to Stretford Shipbreakers, on the Manchester Ship Canal, shortly thereafter.

91. MV DAME CAROLINE HASLETT

Dame Caroline Haslett built in 1950 by Hall, Russell of Aberdeen started out as a standard up-river collier to serve London's few power stations sited above London Bridge. The ships could easily be directed elsewhere as required. North Thames and also South Eastern Gas had very similar dimension ships - the maximum capacity for coal, given tight draught and 'air-draught' under the Thames bridges. As the number of up-river installations reduced, this vessel was converted for the role of underwater electric cable maintenance work. She spent some time moored at the old power station quay in Southwick Canal, between forays out for cable work. The c.1982 photograph gives an indication of the work that had been done to ready the ship for this role. A special bow-lead, small bipod foremast, cable track way and a raised wheelhouse had been fitted over the normal fore hatch area. In 1982, the ship reverted to plain cargo mode, and was renamed *Dame Caroline*. She went to Middlesbrough breakers in 1984.

92. MV BATTERSEA

From the same series as the previous ship, the 1951 built *Battersea* is seen entering Shoreham c.1979, on one of those occasional diversions, from her usual discharge points. With everything above bridge level either telescopic or hinged these ships had evolved over about 50 or 60 years, for their specialised trade. They were, at 2,700 tons by no means small colliers - just 'low-profile'. Dimensions 270ft by 40 ft and 16ft 6in draught. *Battersea* was sold in 1980 to Irish owners, but sank in the Irish Sea in 1981, under the name *Grainville*.

93.1 MV TOTLAND

Grangemouth built in 1952, the 1,570grt *Totland* was a regular to the South Eastern Gas Company's Portslade Works. Similar ships *Lancing* and *Steyning* were also employed, coal arriving in approx 2,000 ton consignments. These ships in common with most colliers of the day had 'tan' or 'collier-brown' upperworks - best suited to constant coal dusty atmosphere. In the 1972 photograph the ship is at the domestic coal wharf. By 1974 *Totland* had departed to foreign flag as *Astroland*. Note the slight hint of streamlining to bridge and funnel.

93.2 MV ZAANSTROOM

An old established Dutch firm, the Holland Steamship Co. began running a twice weekly cargo service to Shoreham in the 1950s. *Zaanstroom*, 496grt built in 1952 was an excellent example of a modern motor cargo liner, for the short sea trades. This ship came from the Westerbroek Shipyard and, like many of her compatriots, to take full advantage of manning levels, she just fell within the 500 tons. Holland Steamship Co. had their own terminal just inside Southwick Locks. In this 1964 photo, the ship is outbound, and not much loaded, by the look of things.

94.1 SS LORD WARDEN

1952 constructed, again a Denny ship, *Lord Warden*, 3,333grt is seen basking in the sunshine at Newhaven Workshops Quay resplendent in blue with the Sealink lettering not greatly enhancing her appearance, c.1970. Displaced by larger vessels on the Dover routes, this ship then relieved on other routes, as required.

94.2 SS LISIEUX

French Railways last conventional steam passenger ferry for the Dieppe route, *Lisieux* at 2,943grt and with a much more streamlined appearance, became running mate to *Brighton* in 1952. Subsequently displaced by the Ro-Ro brigade, she went for further service in the Mediterranean, under the Greek flag and was finally scrapped in 1983 - a fair length career in all. In the photo *Lisieux* is leaving Newhaven for Dieppe still under the old joint railway operation colours.

95.1 MT KITE

One of a large fleet of tugs on the Medway owned by J.P.Knight, the 1952 built 118grt *Kite* is seen here working at Newhaven c.1970 on hopper barge duty. This smart tug came from Richards Shipyard at Lowestoft, and could produce 950 hp.

95.2 M1136, HMS FITTLETON

Deviating briefly from commercial craft, this wooden hulled 'ton' class minesweeper was one of a very large group and was based at the Sussex R.N.R. training facility by Aldrington Basin in about 1975. These vessels displaced 360/425 tons and could manage 15kts on their diesels. Of 152ft by 29ft, on active service their complement was 29. M1136 came from Whites Shipyard.

96.1 and 96.2
MV GLENSHIRA

Scotts of Bowling produced this rather 'chubby' little rnotorship in 1953 as an early replacement example for the fleet of ageing steam 'puffers', those delightful little steamers whose exhaust had originally 'puffed' up the funnel. They were not fitted with condensers in the normal marine manner. At 153grt 190dwt and a mere 86ft by 20ft, *Glenshira* was quite deep draughted for her

size, at 9ft. As motor transport and roll-on, roll-off ferries spread in the Western Isles, *Glenshira* came south to new horizons. Photograph 1. shows her minus her original derrick, still in cargo mode, c.1977 at Aldrington Basin, Shoreham. Photograph 2 has her running into Newhaven, converted for salvage operations c.1980. She has been fitted with sheerlegs, bow roller and winch, and derrick, further aft.

97. SS SIR WILLIAM WALKER

Almost part of the Shoreham scenery for a quarter of a century, this steam collier and three identical sister ships, largely kept the power station supplied with coal from the North East coast. At 2 901grt the 1954 built *Sir William Walker* was the first of the quartet, specially suited to Southwick's 1957 lock. The ships measured 340ft by 44 ft with 18 ft draught. Each ship undertook about fifty or so voyages per year. Far advanced from the earlier collier image, the large domed funnel and streamlined plating to bridge and poop deck sides was as modern looking as ships of this category ever reached. The crew had single berth cabins and a laundry. Since catching the tide was even more important at Shoreham than elsewhere, the ships triple expansion engine together with oil-fired boilers 'Reheat' system, gave a speed of 11 knots - about one knot faster than most colliers of the period. The *Sir William Walker* came from the shipyard of Austin & Pickersgill at Sunderland. At the end of 1983 the ship went to scrap at Bilbao, Spain by which time she had probably carried about 5,000,000 tons of coal. The ship is seen arriving at Shoreham in about 1964, note - Sister ships *James Rowan*, *Sir John Snell* and *Charles H. Merz*. A nearly identical ship, *Sir Johnstone Wright* was built in 1955, but to the Thames '*Cliff Quay*' dimensions.

98. MV GEORGE BOWER and MV JAN HAMM

Dating from 1954, *George Bower* came into service as the Danish United Steamship Company's *Andros*, which raised letter name can still clearly be seen on the bow. Although a motor cargo vessel she was very much of the old type with midships accommodation and a full set of cargo derricks. At 1,810grt, by the time of the 1970 photograph she had moved on to Mediterranean owners and was in general trade to that area. The crew are evidently attempting to spruce up the old ship with staging overside for a lick of paint. *Jan Hamm* is a typical Hamburg built motor coaster of the 1950s, of 424grt, she is waiting for a berth to discharge a cargo of Baltic timber and, judging from the red-lead measles, she too is taking advantage of the enforced wait. In the background, the 1906 power station, no longer generating, awaits the demolition squad. This installation had become known as Brighton 'A' Power Station.

99. SS JAMES ROWAN

The 1955 built *James Rowan* presents a very smart appearance in 1975 for a ship totally dedicated to the coal trade. One of the Shoreham 'quartet', 2,947grt and 3,600dwt. At the end of this ship's 28 year career there was an attempt at preservation, however, she went to breakers at Queenborough, Kent in 1984. Note - the number 73 on the monkey island wood surround. This system of ship numbering applied to all colliers London bound, and had been the main reporting system pre-radio, whereby word could be sent from a special 'collier hailing station' at Tilbury, through the Coal Exchange, to the ultimate destination. The daytime stemming number was backed up by night with horizontal light signals for the up-river flatties, or vertical for others. All red/white/blue in any combination of four.

100. SS JAN TURTLEJSKI/GDY 212

Oceanographic Survey ships are not frequent visitors to Sussex ports, but on one or two occasions a few of these interesting and different craft have appeared, to coincide with Brighton held exhibitions and symposiums on oceanology. This Polish steam research vessel was moored at Southwick for a few days c.1970 and open to the public. The *Jan Turtlejski's* past life had evidently been as a deep sea trawler and she is

typical of the final era of steam in that trade. Trawler owners were among the last to abandon steam reciprocating engines. They were excellent for slow running with the nets out and yet quite capable of a speedy dash to market with the catch. Still carrying her fishing vessel numbers GDY212, the ship's home port was Gdynia.

101. MV DURHAMBROOK

North Quay, Newhaven with a 'full house' in 1961. One little German motor coaster sandwiched between two Brits. The nearest vessel is Comben Longstaff's *Durhambrook* of 1955. Built by De Haan, Heusden, Holland, this 1,275grt motorship sees the beginning of the end for her owner's fleet of steamers. The trend now being to place the bridge aft, although in this case three hatches and derricks were more traditional. In the photograph, if not coal, the likely cargo would have been roadstone from a West Country quarry. Note the very full set of quayside tracked cranes, all rail siding connected. At the far end can be seen *SS Branksome* (see no.86).

102.1 and 102.2 SS ZAPADNAJA DVINA

At 2,491grt, this Finnish built Russian steamer was one of a large number of similar craft specially suited as timber carriers. The design is another variation of the old 'Baltic' type, wide open decks with winches and derricks mounted high for the inevitable deck cargo necessary to load the ship down to her marks. It is interesting to note that this large class of steamship was being constructed at exactly the same period as the last British steam colliers c.1955. *Zapadnaja Dvina* was 289ft by 43ft with 19ft draught. The engine was a quadruple expansion unit. In the 1963 photo the ship had brought timber from Archangel, a regular Russian load port on the White Sea. The later 1975 view shows a solidly built and well maintained ship. Russian crews, at the time, were much larger than their Western counterparts. Who in 1975 would have imagined the 'hammer & sickle' vanishing from the World's oceans?

103.1 MT SHELL WELDER

Shell Welder indicates shipbuilding renewal for the Shell/B.P. combined coastal tanker fleet. Constructed by Clelands at Wallsend, the 569grt tanker often visited Portslade and was photographed in 1964. As in the general scheme of things - by 1974 larger ships started to take over - *Shell Welder*, with minimal name change went to work in the Solent area as a dredger called *Steel Welder* for a few more years.

103.2 SS ADUR

With the major reconstruction of Shoreham Harbour in 1957, the need to maintain deeper navigable channels arose. The steam bucket dredger *Adur* was built in Holland in 1955 and was 199grt at 147ft in length. She was maintained locally in the Adur drydock at Southwick - the old 1855 lock, converted. In the photograph of about 1964 a hopper barge is sandwiched between *Adur* and the harbour tug.

← 104. MV WINSTON

The 13 knot *St. Rognvald* had been a stalwart of the North of Scotland, Orkney and Shetland Shipping Company, since her entry into service in 1955. Another Denny of Dumbarton product, she was powered by a 7 cylinder Sulzer engine. By the time of the c.1980 photograph, the ship had become outmoded by larger Ro-Ro ferries, and went under the Panamanian flag. Still operating a kind of liner service she then ran from Shoreham to the Iberian Peninsula, in company with a few other old British coasters finally meeting the breakers in 1998 on the Canary Islands. A long career indeed for the 1024grt *St.Rognvald*.

← 105. M V WERA

By the mid 1950s, the West German coastal fleet was being totally reconstructed. Several shipyards produced many very efficient motor coasters, especially in the 300-500 ton range. They were able, very quickly to make large inroads into the Northern European coastal trades, and none more so than the timber trade from the Baltic. Rendsburg built and registered, the 421grt *Wera* is a typical example of these attractive little vessels. Still part riveted in construction, radar had yet to be fitted. In this c.1967 photo at the Outer Layby , Shoreham, a good deck load of Baltic timber awaits the stevedores.

106. ARUNDEL

This 1956 built steam collier for Stephenson, Clarke came from the Sunderland shipyard of Austin and Pickersgill. At 3,422grt and 4,600dwt, the 344ft long *Arundel* exceeded the regular callers length by a few feet, and was deeper draughted at 20ft, making occasional extra spring tide visits on the local coal brigade. No steam colliers were built during or after 1957 and *Arundel*, it would appear, had been a candidate for more general trading, judging by the mast derrick supports and winch platforms. Nevertheless, the coal trade was her mainstay until, surplus to requirements in 1972, she went to Italy as *Brick Dodecesimo*, trading for a further 10 years there before scrapping in 1982. The 1970 scene at the Power Station quay, Southwick, shows just how large the local electricity generation industry had become. *Sir William Walker* and *James Rowan* lie astern of *Arundel*, in differing stages of discharge. Given a full complement of shore cranes, one of these large colliers would be turned round in one tide. Between them, over 11,000 tons of coal would have gone ashore. Note - to highlight the progression in ship types and propulsion, no further coastal steamers appear.

107.1 and 107.2
MV PICONEGRO,
MV PICOGRIS, MV
PICOMAR

No less than three members of the Spanish L.S.Mino Fleet were captured here in 1970, just inside Southwick locks. All were regular traders with general cargo, wines and sherry. The fact that three appeared at once may have been due to gale delays or the Christmas rush. *Piconegro* at 1,445grt was the largest, *Picogris* b.1957 and *Picomar* b.1953 were 600 tons apiece. The 1967 photograph is interesting, apart from the crewman making sure his mate leaves 'no holidays' in the red lead, the solid construction riveted throughout is clearly seen. Also are clinker built lifeboats. With the Bay of Biscay on the menu every few days, *Piconegro* needed to be of stout stuff. The A.S.Mino fleet was built and owned at Bilbao.

108.1 and 108.2 MV IVY B.

This 1956 built, 350grt, motor coaster is distinctly an ex-Dutch vessel. A number of 'schoots' as they were termed, came to the British flag, as the Netherlands fleet tended towards larger units. *Ivy B*, joined Van Broek of London. In this 1980 photograph she is entering drydock at Southwick for some underwater attention. (It was the old 1855 lock). Whether the 'crumple' on the stern was relevant or not, is unknown.

109. MV BUENOS AIRES STAR

In the late 1960s Fisher & Duforrest opened a large cargo terminal just inside Newhaven Harbour, especially for the import of perishable produce - fruit, veg, meat etc. and for some years surprisingly large ocean going ships called. Many of these were of the refrigerated cargo type, this development was something quite out of the ordinary for the Sussex scene, *Buenos Aires Star,* 8,257grt, needs little introduction to those familiar with the Deep Sea trades. Built in 1956, this Blue Star Line vessel was almost at the end of her career, being scrapped in Taiwan, shortly thereafter. The Newhaven scene is c.1980.

110.1 MV KIRTONDYKE ↗

Seen discharging coal at Southwick's Turberville Wharf in 1970, this ship, although not unusual, does illustrate the diversity of shipyards and indeed shipowners, of the period. *Kirtondyke*, 959grt, was a product of Hayes Yard, Pembroke Dock in Wales. She was owned by Klondyke Shipping of Hull.

110.2 MV BRANDON →

Brandon, 586grt, came from Charles Hill's Bristol Shipyard in 1957, and was a smaller type of collier. The ship's earlier career for Osborne and Wallis, had largely been in the Bristol Channel coal trade. In the photo c.1980 she was running to Shoreham. In 1989 scrapping took place at Lisbon.

111. MV BELGIA

Reflecting the trends of the time this smart Belgian built and owned cargo vessel has some streamlining yet still with the old midships accommodation design. The cargo gear consists of both the old and new in terms of a pair of kingposts with derricks, but new electric deck cranes elsewhere. The forward crane appears to carry a lightweight pole mast to support the steaming light. *Belgia*, 1,496grt, built in 1957, and a near sister of the Swedish *Gertrude Bratt,* operated to the Baltic in general and paper trades. These ships were ice strengthened and needed to be in the Baltic winters. The photograph c.1965 shows *Belgia* departing from the Prince Philip Lock at Southwick.

112. MV BERND GUNDA →

Pastel shades were becoming increasingly popular, especially in Continental fleets during the 1950s. The 1957 built *Bernd Gunda* was an excellent example of the West German coastal fleet, making many voyages with Baltic timber. In 1968 this 387grt ship carried one such load to Littlehampton. Always immaculately kept, often to find a return freight to the north, ships of this type would first go down channel in ballast to one of the West Country china clay ports. The photograph dates from 1967.

113.1 and 113.2 MV WALTER RICHTER/WATERDALE

Another German coaster which often visited Sussex ports over many years was the 1957 built, 423grt, *Walter Richter*. She differed from many of her contemporaries by having a small extra post and derrick amidships. In 1972 she came to grief entering Newhaven, going aground just in Seaford Bay. In due course cargo was removed, the ship saved, and brought into Newhaven Harbour. Later she re-emerged under the Red Ensign as *Waterdale*, being placed under the care of Rye Shipping Ltd. With masts now devoid of derricks as was the trend, she then relied entirely on shore craneage. Photograph 1 leaving the River Adur in 1967 and photograph 2 shows her at sea in new livery. Later *Waterdale* went under the St. Vincent flag as *Sandy*.

114.1 MV ARABRITT

A2, 999grt Swedish cargo ship built in 1957 *Arabritt* is seen arriving at Shoreham in 1965, with a part cargo of British Columbian timber. A voyage of some 8,500 miles, via the Panama Canal. Over several years a number of large Norwegian, Swedish and German ships in the 4,000dwt range were in this trade. *Arabritt's* cargo gear has evolved to bi-pod masts and the 'all-aft' layout is becoming more popular. The ship was built at Landskrona and owned in Stockholm by A.R.Appelqvist. *Arabritt* and sister ship *Arabert* were subsequently lengthened.

114.2 MV PEN DART

Purpose built for the sand and ballast trade as a suction dredger, by P.K.Harris of Appledore, Devon, the 499grt *Sand Dart* operated along the South Coast. About five years after her 1957 construction, the ship grounded in thick fog on the Dorset coast - this in pre-radar days. A protracted, but successful, salvage operation followed and when in service again she traded as *Pen Dart*. The 1964 photo shows a small platform just above the funnel on the mainmast - ready for the radar scanner to be fitted. This would keep her clear of further such embarrassments.

115. MV CON ZELO

Spaandam, Holland in 1957 was the birthplace of this smart little 400 tonner. She came to the Red Ensign later and a long association with Sussex ports began. Often the ship carried beech-boules, logs sliced horizontally but banded together, for use in the manufacture of furniture. These came from Northern France and the trade was an old one. In the photograph c.1976 the Shoreham Pilot has just disembarked and it looks to be set fair for the return leg across the Channel.

116. MV HERON

A more modern member of the General Steam Navigation Company's fleet, the 943grt *Heron* came from the Bristol Shipyard of Charles Hill in 1957. In the 1968 scene she is moored at that Company's Aldrington Basin terminal whilst serving their Bay of Biscay trade. *Heron* was very traditional in both layout and cargo gear fitted, nevertheless had an extremely pleasing design. (see Drake) The white hulled ship astern of *Heron* is the West German Horn Lines *Stadt Schleswig*, of 1958 and 428grt operating in the fruit trades.

117. MV HUMPHREY GILBERT

No, not a reduced Dieppe ferry! With a gross tonnage all of 35, but a true British Rail ferry, the *Humphrey Gilbert* was en-route in 1977 to the Thames from the River Dart. She was undoubtedly fine running the Kingswear to Dartmouth ferry service, but it proved a bit too much to ask such a small ship to operate on the lower reaches of the Thames. This did not succeed. It is rather unlikely that she tested Newhaven's Marine Engineers too drastically - compared to cross channel ferries and I.O.W. paddle steamers.

118. MV AMETHYST / FAITH

The Scottish firm of William Robertson, Shipowners, otherwise known as Gem Line had owned steam coasters long ago. By the 1950s motor coasters formed the fleet, and in 1958 they took delivery of *Amethyst,* 1,548grt, from Ailsa Shipbuilding at Troon. In the 1980 photograph *Amethyst* has just delivered her last consignment of coal to Southwick, and with change of name and flag, is seen departing for horizons new as *Faith,* under Panamanian control. One of the jobs soon facing the new owners would be to erase the Robertson identifier white line, painted on the hull below the bridge. This had been on Robertson's ships for decades, even after their 1978 integration with Stephenson, Clarke.

119. MV QUEENSLAND

Originally built for the Newbigin Steamship Company of Newcastle as *Greathope*, this 2,750grt vessel was geared for general trading, but spent much time in the coal trade. As *Greathope* she visited Shoreham power station and being of very similar dimensions to the Electricity Board colliers presumably made her an attractive 'extra' to their fleet. By 1965 the ship changed hands to Shipping & Coal, but visits continued as before. Austin and Pickersgill at Sunderland must have made the old ship of stout stuff, for she subsequently traded under eight different names, before sinking in 1989. In the 1965 photograph, the *Queensland* is arriving with more coal and by this time her derricks, un-rigged, were permanently lashed to the cross-trees out of use.

120. MT PETWORTH →

The second *Petworth* to appear in Stephenson, Clarke's fleet, this version was a 1,266grt motor tanker. The design is very streamlined, as was the general trend for ships in 1958. Built by Clelands, (successors) Ltd., Wallsend on Tyne, *Petworth* was powered by a 7 cylinder British Polar Diesel engine. In 1978 she went to Greek owners for further service and was not broken up until 1989 in Turkey. The 1973 photograph sees her leaving the River Adur in front of the Lifeboat slipway, having part discharged at Shoreham.

121. MV RON WOOLAWAY →

Built in 1958 as a standard Dutch coaster design, this ship's first name was *Skelskar*. Shortly after, she was converted to the dredging trade to operate in the Bristol Channel area, whereupon a serious mishap occurred. The 478grt ship 'turned-turtle' in the Bristol Channel with a major stability problem. In due course the ship was righted, repaired and modified, before returning to trade. The extent of the modifications can clearly be seen in the 1965 photo of the ship departing Newhaven. From beneath the forecastle, a special fore and aft blister tank had been fitted, port and starboard, extending to beneath the bridge area. This gave the ship a strange end-on profile, and of course increased the beam. Ordeal behind her, the *Ron Woolaway* moved to Sussex and, still bearing Barnstaple as port of registry, she resumed trading without further mishap as a result of those buoyancy tanks. Later she joined South Coast as *Sand Finch*.

122. MV STORRINGTON

At 3,809grt the 1959 built *Storrington* came from the Burntisland Shipyard, in Scotland. The ship is particularly interesting as she was in essence the final midships accommodation type collier, ever built. The deadweight capacity of this ship was 5,000 tons. The overall dimensions were a little greater at 345ft by 49ft compared to the collier fleets, but this ship was fitted with a full set of winches and derricks for general trading. In earlier years the traditional collier 'tan' paintwork had been applied, but in this 1978 scene in Southwick Canal, white had been substituted, and since the quarantine flag is flying, this was not a coal or coastal voyage. The Newhaven tug *Metrec* has the bow line. Not long after this time *Storrington* became *Milos II*, under the Cypriot flag.

123. MV SHEKSNALES / MV SAND GULL

The 1959 built 534grt *Sand Gull* had one visible design alteration from her earlier sisters - that of a full width, totally enclosed, bridge. In this 1970 photograph she is heading towards Southwick Locks from the ballast Wharf at Portslade, en-route to the Channel for the next cargo. The ship traded along the South Coast until 1992 when she was scrapped. Behind *Sand Gull* lies a lot of hard work waiting for the local stevedores, in the form of a full cargo of timber aboard the 1964 built Russian MV *Sheksnales* 2,921grt. This vessel represents a new class of Russian timber carrier, the bridge and accommodation having been sited 'two thirds aft', one step nearer the 'all aft' design almost universal subsequently. This class of ship would trade anywhere in the World where a cargo was on offer.

← 124.1 MV HUMBER LEE

The 616grt *Humber Lee* was originally I.C.I.'s motor coaster *Calcium* of 1959. Converted to a suction dredger, as seen in this c.1978 scene, she was discharging at Newhaven's only west bank commercial quay. This has now disappeared.

↙ 124.2 MV RYE TRADER

At 200grt, originally *Queensgate* then *Polarlight*, the 118 ft *Rye Trader* was one of many similar sized craft built c.1959. By 1971 she was in the hands of Rye Shipping. Masts were becoming scarce as well as derricks, with total reliance on shore cranes, and *Rye Trader* has but a thin pole to support the steaming light and a flag halyard. These ships were well suited to 'under the bridges' trading and for shallow river channels.

125. MV ROYA

Representing a smaller class of standard Russian cargo ship, *Roya* 1,211grt was twin screw fitted and of relatively shallow draught. Built in 1959 a number of the class visited Sussex ports in the sixties and seventies with the inevitable timber cargo. The photograph at Kingston Wharf on the River Adur is of some historic background interest as this site was one of the original cross channel ferry terminals - c.1840s. Kingston even had its own railway station, demolished in 1879, as the passenger traffic went to Newhaven, forsaking both Shoreham and Littlehampton. Kingston Railway Wharf, just to the left in the picture continued as a freight wharf, connected to the main railway line.

126.1 MV DORSET COAST

Ardrossan built in 1959, this 1,125grt vessel had been part of the enormous Coast Lines group of companies, and as such she operated variously around the U.K, on their liner services. In 1974 she moved from the Belfast Steamship Company to General Steam Navigation. The 1974 view is at Aldrington Basin, the ship having a plain black funnel at this time. In 1980 she went to Egypt for further service.

126.2 MT ESSO IPSWICH

The 1960 built *Esso Ipswich*, 1,103grt, shows the ship unit size to be increasing. *Esso Ipswich* visited Aldrington's Esso terminal and in this 1977 photograph a part discharge would appear to have taken place, the ship heading out via the 1957 lock. Wine tanks are stacked nearby.

127.1 and 127.2 MT MEECHING

P.K.Harris of Appledore built a large number of similar looking tugs for various owners in the late 1950s and early 60s. British Railways took delivery of *Meeching* for Newhaven towage and salvage duties. *Meeching's* twin uptakes in lieu of a conventional funnel appeared quite radical in design at the time. The 160grt tug could produce 1,040bhp and came to serve Newhaven for forty years, sometimes being involved in major salvage operations in the English Channel. In the 1964 photograph she is engaged in the essential, but more mundane job, of handling mud hoppers for the dredger. In the 1978 scene, *Meeching* is assisting at Shoreham, on ship towage duty.

← 128.1 MT KINGSTON BUCI

Surely one of the most attractive designed harbour tugs, the 76grt *Kingston Buci* clearly shows the 'family' origin of the type. From the same Devon shipyard, she was almost a half size version of *Meeching*, capable of any kind of harbour towage duty. The 1970 scene in Shoreham entrance has the tug towing the mud hoppers to sea, the blue cranes of Kingston Railway Wharf visible in the background. Like *Meeching*, this vessel was also fitted for fire fighting, the nozzle being canvas covered on the monkey island. After twenty years at Shoreham she went to Poole as *Kingston Lacy*.

↙ 128.2 OLGA. K

The 1978 Shoreham entrance photo is less common a sight showing a large Greek 'logger', the *Olga K*. With the assistance of *Kingston Buci* and *Meeching*, the 2,982grt ship is about to be eased around the bend by *Kingston Buci* whilst *Meeching's* greater power will provide the braking force astern.. Both tugs were built in 1960.

129. SS HARDWICKE GRANGE

Houlder Brothers' *Hardwicke Grange* at 10,338grt was steam turbine powered, a few deep sea cargo ships being engined in this way right into the early 1960s. The ship was built in 1961 by Hawthorn, Leslie of Newcastle, and had a refrigerated cargo capacity of 439,000cu.ft. and passenger accommodation for twelve. The service speed being 16 knots. At 489ft in length she was a very large ship indeed to visit Newhaven, c.1977, and evidently the discharge is progressing utilising ship's union purchase derrick gear - the Railway cranes were simply not tall enough to plumb her holds. Despite her well cared for appearance, *Hardwicke Grange* could compete not much longer, she went to scrap in 1979 as the Liberian flag *Jacques*, a very short career for a classic British cargo liner.

130. MV DESEADO

At 11,248grt and 510ft in length, Royal Mail Lines *Deseado* was another 'ocean giant' by Newhaven or Sussex standards. The 1980 visit to East Quay again shows cargo being worked by union purchase derrick system. The Cammell Laird, 1961 built ship was a 17 knot motor vessel and therefore stood a better chance of competing longer than the previous vessel. This ship had 400,000 cu. ft. of refrigerated cargo space and had started life as Shaw, Saville's *Iberic*, taking up Royal Mail Lines livery in 1977.

131.1 MT ESSO DOVER ↗

This smart little coastal tanker built in 1961 was 490grt and shows the continuing modernisation of the Esso fleet. Note the top of the funnel, streamlined into the mainmast. The foremast is the same kind of section allowing rung access aloft on the after side, it is largely unstayed except for a forestay to hoist the anchor signal, on its halyard. An array of T.V. aerials is fitted aft for the crew's off duty moments. *Esso Dover* was a very frequent visitor to Shoreham in the early 1960s. In 1981 she was sold, becoming *Cherrybobs*, *Bosun Bird* and finally *Al Reen*, in Kenyan waters.

131.2 MT ESSO JERSEY →

A mere 121ft by 24ft and 10ft draught, this tiny oil tanker at 313grt was built for the Turf Lock dimensions on the Exeter Ship Canal in 1962. Presumably she would have been called *Esso Exeter*, but for the existence of an ocean going ship of the same name. Another frequent Shoreham visitor in the 1960s, she later became the *John S. Derbyshire* and finally was dismantled at Hull. The 1964 photograph shows the ship almost discharged at a Portslade terminal.

132. ANN M

Metcalf Motor Coasters built up a fleet perfectly described by the Company name over several decades. The 1,203grt *Ann M* came from the Burntisland Shipyard on the Firth of Forth in 1962. After a maiden voyage with coal to Shoreham, she settled into a specialist trade carrying steelworks slag to the Tarmac Plant on the River Adur at Shoreham. *Ann M*, *Melissa M.* and *Christopher M.* were often engaged in carrying roadstone also, and there were still plenty of coal cargoes to be had in the 1960s. Unusually in the 1979 photograph the ship is moored just inside Southwick Locks. After changing hands she traded as *Whitburn*, then *Ann II*, before reaching Garston shipbreakers in 1994 - a good length career.

133.1 MV ATHENE ↗

In the early 1960s, long before settling at Portsmouth and the introduction of Ro-Ro ferries, the Channel Islands traffic had been largely the preserve of British Railways cargo vessels. As conventional services altered, Commodore Shipping ran small cargo coasters on a variety of routes e.g. to Kingston Wharf, Shoreham and Rainham. Also they became very involved with seasonal trades from the Channel Islands, often chartering Dutch and German ships for such peaks as the tomato crop. In this 1968 photograph, the West German 1962 built, 499grt *Athene* has unloaded at Aldrington Basin. Sporting her charterers lion symbol on their bright blue funnel, *Athene* has already lost her two after derricks in deference to shore craneage.

133.2 MV ERNA OLDENDORFF →

Egon Oldendorff, an old established German Company, started to replace their steamers with new tonnage in the 1950s. Seen in the 1965 photo with more British Columbian timber at the Inner Lay-by, Southwick, is *Erna Oldendorff*, 2,983grt 4,335dwt built at Lubeck in 1962. She replaced a 1916 steamer of the same name. A full conventional set of cargo gear is fitted.

134. MV FORT CREVECOUER

Apart from cross channel traffic, visiting French cargo ships were not that common a sight in Sussex, despite their proximity just over the horizon. The refrigerated *Fort Crevecouer*, 5,020grt makes a variation berthed at Newhaven's East Quay in 1977. Clearly visible along the ship's hull are side doors, used often in the banana and fruit trades, in which this ship operated. Owned by the French Line (CGT) *Fort Crevecouer* was likely to have been a Dieppe regular from the Caribbean area. The ship has the typical 'reefer' layout of the day, with bipod type masts, large deck houses, etc. and possibly carried a few passengers from time to time. She was built in 1962.

135. MV MAGUELONE

Wine tankers, by virtue of their trade were never exactly numerous. Both Newhaven and Shoreham had bulk wine storage tanks as the Nations' taste for such delights grew. Previously wines and sherries were shipped mostly in casks and then large metal containers. The French owned *Maguelone*, 1,833grt was, in fact, a partial wine tanker carrying general goods in the holds, but with additional large tank spaces given over to the stowage of bulk wine. The ship was built in 1963. In the 1976 photo the ship appears only to have pumped a small consignment to the Shoreham tanks. Over *Maguelone's* No 2 hatch an approaching CEGB collier is waiting for the empty lock.

← 136. MT SW2

A smart little motor tanker built to the same dimensions as the *Esso Jersey*, S.W.2, 245grt, carried 'effluent' on behalf of the South Western Water Authority, in the Exeter area. The 1963 built ship is seen in the photo drydocking at Southwick c1970s. Later this vessel was given the name *Countess of Wear* in 1975. In the background the dredger *Adur* and tug *Kingston Buci*, beyond the drydock gate, are, of course, at 'canal level'.

137. MV DICTION

The 1963 built *Diction* represents a very large number of similar sized craft constructed for her owners in the 1950s and 60s. The London & Rochester Shipping Company had run Thames barges, auxiliaries and motor coasters for many years. *Diction* was 189grt. Ships such as *Diction* were in no small way replacements for the ageing fleet of wooden barges. This new type of motor coastal barge could still go to up-river and shallow estuarial berths as visited in such numbers by the old sailing barges. Nevertheless, craft like *Diction* were perfectly capable of making coastal and near continental voyages. Many of these delightful little ships were still in service scattered far and wide by the year 2000. *Diction* was photographed in the eastern extremity of Aldrington Basin in 1973. The ship's foremast light arrangement still seems to be the old 'haul aloft by lanyard' method. London & Rochester were also known as Crescent Shipping and had a crescent moon on the funnel, the reddish brown hulls are another feature easily recognisable.

138. MV FRIVOLITY

F.T.Everard & Sons also replaced some of their old barges with modern versatile little motor coasters. The 199grt *Frivolity* and sister ship *Festivity* of 1963 being good examples. Although traditionally derrick rigged, this c.1964 photograph shows the hatch cover arrangements have been updated to mechanical sliding type. On occasion, towards the end of exporting cement from Asham on the River Ouse, one of these little ships journeyed above Newhaven to that remote quay.

139. RRS JOHN MURRAY

Built in 1963 as a stern trawler, this vessel was specially converted for the work of the National Environmental Research Council. *John Murray* is fitted with laboratories and workshops geared for geological seabed surveys, etc and the 441grt ship was present at Shoreham c.1970 for a few days during an Oceanology conference at Brighton. In later years the ship appeared in a bright orange livery - this did not do a lot for her appearance, but would have made the ship eminently more visible at sea. Note the small aftermast bearing tiny gaff and the Blue Ensign, between the twin exhaust uptakes. At 133ft 6in in length, she was not required to carry the second steaming light. R.R.S. means Royal Research Ship.

140.1. MT BOLTON

Photographed entering the River Adur in 1977 is Bowker & King's 495grt motor tanker *Bolton*. With a high forecastle and poop, the maindeck would still be mostly awash on loaded trips, in all but calm seas. *Bolton* went to the Greek flag in 1985.

140.2 MT HAMBLE

At 1,182grt *Hamble*, named after Shell/B.P.'s distribution facility on Southampton Water, was built in 1964. The ship carries her combined owners' emblems above the wheelhouse doors. Two small davit-like cranes handle the hose connections, and a light derrick is fitted to the foremast for stores, etc. The 1970 scene has the coastguard station beyond the grassy mound of the old fort, on Shoreham Beach, between the ship's mast and bridge.

141. MV CAPELLA

The State controlled shipping company of the East German Democratic Republic operated a large fleet of motor coasters in three or four distinct size classes. Seen departing Shoreham in 1971, the 617grt, *Capella* was registered in Rostock. This vessel sometimes brought Baltic timber to Sussex, and is about to drop the Pilot, as several members of the crew gaze wistfully at the receding shoreline. Although fitted with the latest electric cranes for cargo work, Capella still has tarpaulin hatch covers, wooden wedges and rope lashings over traditional boards.

142. MV FRIGG

Owned by Linde, of Sweden, this colourful cargo-ship built in 1965 is seen entering the River Adur in 1970.
At 499grt, the ship's deck cargo of timber can be seen to be composed of 'banded ' stacks, not solidly stowed.
The old order in the timber trade was changing - standards of loose timber becoming metricated and packaged.
With the blue and yellow Swedish flag fluttering astern, *Frigg* is heading to an up-river berth beyond the 'scotch-derrick' railway cranes on Kingston Wharf. Note - Blue, with the advance of more sophisticated ship's paint systems, would become more and more popular - almost 'the new black' in the maritime world.

143. MV RYNSTROOM

The Holland Steamship Company's advanced new type of general cargo carrier *Rynstroom* is seen at that Company's Southwick Terminal, in 1970. In the search for economy and speed of operation, this old established firm ordered *Rynstroom* for their Holland/Shoreham service in 1965. Using side doors, ramps and lifts, loading and unloading could be achieved with the use of pallets and fork lift trucks. This ship had no conventional hatches, was constructed at Arnhem, and of 500grt. An 1,800hp diesel gave a speed of 14 knots. This made *Rynstroom* a very efficient operator but, despite this major attempt to modernise short sea cargo handling, it was not enough - containerisation and Ro-Ro proved the winners in the end. *Rynstroom* and the once proud Holland Steamship Company ceased trading just a few years later.

← 144.1 MV GABROVO

A very rare ensign to be seen in Sussex, and not that often elsewhere, is that of Bulgaria. In 1982, the general cargo ship *Gabrovo* of the Bulgarian State Shipping Company visited Shoreham. Built in 1965, the 1,698grt vessel was very traditionally fitted with a full set of cargo derricks. *Gabrovo* probably mostly traded from North West Europe to her Communist homeland.

↙ 144.2 MV JEMRIX

Rix Shipping of Hull had run steam coasters for years and like many operators changed over to motor ships. *Jemrix*, 843grt had started as *Irishgate* before joining their fleet. The ship has the modern steel hatch covers and no cargo gear at all. She was built in 1965. The photograph was taken in 1982.

145. MV EDWARD STONE

Eddystone Shipping's *Edward Stone*, 196grt 295dwt, seen at Rye's Strand Quay c.1965, loading cereals by elevator ex truck. This is at the extreme top end of navigation on the River Tillingham, and the ship has been turned a little way downstream in order to leave the berth laden and 'facing the right way'. Shipments of this nature were somewhat seasonal, and once the new, larger capacity cargo wharf was built at Rye Harbour in the years following, few commercial ships percolated this far. The Quay is now yacht and tourist orientated, hundreds of years of cargo shipping have moved on. By the quayside puddles and coated workers, they are trying to dodge the showers whilst loading from a well tarpaulined lorry. *Edward Stone* was operated by the Lapthorn Company of Hoo, Kent.

← 146. MV VALENCAY

The French partner on the Newhaven - Dieppe route brought in this 5,477grt roll-on, roll-off motor ferry into operation in 1965. Built by Chantiers at St.Nazaire, *Valencay* and her sister vessel *Villandry* were purpose built for vehicular traffic, not converts, and therefore a more modern image arrived for this route. Photographed going astern to the ramp at Newhaven in 1970, the old scheme of things had not entirely gone - *Valencay* still has a fair sized fore hatch, seen open, for baggage and light goods stowage.

← 147. MV FREE ENTERPRISE II

Not a regular at Newhaven, the 4,122grt Townsend Thoresen's Dover based *Free Enterprise II* was briefly running to Dieppe in 1980. This 1965 built roll-on, roll-off motor ferry had both bow and stern doors. The brightly coloured hull and overall design could not, at the time, be called 'classic', the opening bow visor is clearly visible but the smooth flowing lines of the older ferries was giving way to maximising car deck/carrying space and height for the ever growing number of long distance trucks carried. Four Smit - MAN diesels gave 11,550 bhp, and a speed of 21 knots, a little less than the Railway passenger only steamers. Difficult to believe today, but upon their introduction in 1965 this class of vessel was the largest on the Channel routes.

148. MT BEECHCROFT

Another unit of Bowker & King's coastal and estuarial tanker fleet, this little ship presents an up-river appearance very similar to that of the flat-iron colliers already described. 1966 built, the 556grt *Beechcroft* has hinged masts and everything else above wheelhouse level would be removable (there's not much), enabling the ship to pass beneath Thames and other bridges. Perfectly capable of coastwise voyages, *Beechcroft* was bound for the River Adur in 1978.

149. MV PERSEY III

Another 1970 visitor to the Oceanology Exhibition at Brighton, was the 2,289grt Murmansk based Russian research ship *Persey III*, seen leaving at the end of the show, from the Prince Philip Lock. Ships of this type operated Worldwide on surveying, seismic and oceanographic work, plus fishery research, and would stay at sea for long periods. Judging by the rows of portholes, *Persey III* had a large crew and scientific staff to carry out her duties. The ship was built in 1968.

150. MV YANTARNYI →

Staying with Russian shipping, the 2,850grt timberman *Yantarnyi* is seen arriving at Shoreham in 1980 with a large 'packaged' cargo from Northern Russia. With vertical timbers the regulatory 10ft apart, to prevent the load shifting, side ropes for crew safety and the individual package banding, the whole looks very neat and secure. Built in 1968, this bi-pod masted class of cargo ship also had the ability to handle quite heavy loads - one heavy lift derrick being fitted to serve number three hatch. As with all Russian ships, the name is translated from the Cyrillic alphabet to English on a varnished board over the wheelhouse. Despite the big deck load and holds full, the ship is barely down to the marks.

Note - with no further sail or steam powered vessels being described within this book, the motor vessel (MV) is now dropped.

151. ATHINA B →

Not for a long time had Brighton witnessed such a large off-peak tourist attraction as in January 1980. Struggling to make port in a gale the Greek freighter *Athina B* got into difficulties off Shoreham, finally having to be abandoned. By some peculiar dint of good fortune she finally came ashore just east of Palace Pier, Brighton, avoiding same in the process. Duly her cargo of pumice was unloaded on the beach, and Eurosalve Ltd managed to refloat her. However, at a mere 12 years of age, the ship evidently wasn't up to much, and she was towed away to the Medway for scrapping, running aground again just before the scrap berth. *Athina B* was a fairly standard build of Japanese design. One very distinct trademark of all Japanese tonnage being the twin tubular or sometimes lattice radio masts right aft on the boat deck. *Athina B* - 1,940grt.

152.1 ACCLIVITY

Built in 1968 was F.T.Everard & Sons, 299grt tanker seen at Portslade the same year. Although small by the standards of the time she is another of those craft much suited to up-river or under the bridges work having little 'air-draught', lowerable masts and low profile.

152.2 FENCHURCH

Gracechurch Lines ran to the Mediterranean on a cargo liner basis and in the 1980 photograph at Southwick, the 1,460grt *Fenchurch* is loading general cargo in the literal sense, including vehicles for export and heavy machinery. *Fenchurch* dated from 1968.

153.1 LEADSMAN

Representing unit size growth in C.Rowbotham's coastal tanker fleet, the 1968 built, 843grt *Leadsman*, shows another feature increasingly prevalent - the general reduction in the size of ship's accommodation blocks. This trend was coming about by the automation of engine rooms, and general crew number being smaller, from the regulatory point of view. *Leadsman* later became *Alston*.

153.2 EURCO FAITH

A number of Greek owners purchased ex Japanese built cargo ships c.1970. They were all solidly built and had heavy cargo gear making for ideal 'loggers' and timbermen. The 1968 built *Eurco Faith*, 3,784grt wears an East African Lines funnel, as she discharges in Shoreham Eastern Arm in 1977.

154. DESTEL

The 1,217grt *Destel* shows the transitional start to full container ship design. Although unable to carry a full width timber deck cargo, hatch tops can still support a good load. If working in the container trades, this ship would be able to stow 90 full sized boxes above and below the hatch covers. This particular West German ship has an interesting feature in the presence of an additional small wheelhouse, up on the monkey island. This second conning position would also be useful navigating in Baltic ice, as well as peering over a stack of containers. Note the fore and aft crew safety lines to the forecastle and plastic sheeting supposedly covering the deck cargo - timber importers were growing less keen on soggy, salted timber. The photograph dates from 1970 and the ship from 1969. The 'G' flag is flying - "pilot requested".

155. SAND SWIFT

South Coasts' 1,085grt 1969 built *Sand Swift* was photographed setting off from Newhaven in 1978 for another load. Despite the abrasive nature of their sand and ballast cargoes, and permanently wet state of the decks, these ships were always smartly kept. In the photo *Sand Swift* has passed the French freight Ro-Ro *Capitaine Le Goff*, and beyond the dredger the masts of the small reefer *Barrad Wave*, can be seen.

156. CHICHESTER CITY

John Heaver's 'Chichester' ships were new to the ballast trade c.1970, but soon a small fleet was operating. The dredgers were quite beamy for their size 39ft, but with an overall length of 200ft could turn in the River Arun, off the Company's Littlehampton Wharf. They were of approx. 1,000grt with a deadweight of 1,700 tons. Later with general Company changes -

Chichester City	was renamed	*City of Chichester*
Chichester Star	"	*City of Portsmouth*
Chichester Cross	"	*Bowcross* (went to Wales)

The view from Littlehamptons' swingbridge c.1978, has *Chichester City* ready for sea, whilst the *Star* has started discharging. The site is of great historical interest as it was from here in the 1860s that the Littlehampton, Havre and Honfleur Steamship Co., started cross channel services. In 1865, the London, Brighton and South Coast Railway Co, took over, and by 1878 all passenger services had gone eastwards to the port of Newhaven. Rail freight traffic, however, continued for about another 100 years. Note one large rail-mounted dockside crane survives in 1978.

↙ 157. JUNIOR

This rather 'ribby' looking basic coaster was one of a series from c.1970 under the guise of XL-400. At 199grt they could lift a good 400 tons of cargo, making for a very economic operation at the time. Several shipowners ran vessels of this class, the *Lady Sandra* was owned by Thomas Watson & Co. and had been built at Wivenhoe. Later becoming *Junior* under the Maltese flag, the ship is seen in the 1987 photograph leaving the River Adur. *Junior* was scrapped in 1988 - a far too short career.

158. ULIDIA

The 1970 built, British Rail, *Ulidia* clearly shows the way forward in design, namely large, floating, box-like, but colourful. At 1,599grt this vessel's hull is simply made to maximise the number of trucks loaded therein. Another trend which appears to have come to stay is the use of ship sides to advertise - still, at least *Ulidia* is conventionally named. In the 1980 photograph the ship looks very smart lying at the Railway Quay at Newhaven. She went to Greece in 1982 as *Autotrader*.

159. EXXTOR I

Since the start of Roll-on, Roll-off ferry operations a great variety of ferries have seen service on the Newhaven - Dieppe route. The 1970 built *Exxtor I*, registered in Jersey was of 1,599grt and typical of the smaller end of the size scale for these ships. Note the maximum width given to the stern door, and deck space given over to truck/trailer parking. The photograph dates from 1980.

160. Strand Quay, Rye c.1970

The huge improvements made in the 1930's by steel piling can be clearly seen. The grey sluice gate to the River Tillingham is over the other side of the main South Coast road, between the two trees. That river navigation was much used by barges up to c.1920s for many miles inland to deliver coal and bring produce back down river to Rye. Extreme right the old gasometer is still there, but it has been a long time since gasworks coal came in by sailing barge. For earlier views at this location look back to *Mountsfield* of 1890, *Anna* 1909, and for reverse *Evelyn* 1900 and *Edward Stone*, c.1965.

← 161. SCHIAFFINO

For a short period the French company, Schiaffino operated a freight only roll-on, roll-off service from Shoreham to Dieppe, from a terminal in Aldrington Basin c.1977. *Schiaffino* belonged to a group of similar vessels which could operate on any of the burgeoning roll-on, roll-off routes. The Cherbourg registered ship is seen leaving Shoreham in 1977. She was built in 1970. Sadly, the Shoreham venture ceased and probably the tide and lock based operation at Shoreham was not best suited for this kind of trade as same time, daily transits would simply be unachievable.

162. The Royal Sovereign Light Tower

NN 87, the fishing vessel *Wildflower*, returns from presumably an angling trip, judging by the numbers onboard. The 1970 photograph, with Seaford in the background, is included specially, since rising construction work on the base column and cabin of the replacement for the Royal Sovereign Lightship is clearly visible. The construction work, just east of Newhaven's east breakwater, is well advanced and in line with NN 87's bow can be seen the light tower/accommodation module, whilst just to the right a crane sits atop the concrete base structure. In the summer of 1970, the whole ensemble was taken out to the shoal, a few miles south east of Beachy Head, and duly assembled and commissioned. The Royal Sovereign Lightship was no more. see *Chrianie*, 1944. There was no mystery about Newhavens' tower.

163. TROUP HEAD

The red, white and blue colours of Christian Salvesens' *Troup Head*, 1,599grt, built in 1971, add some brightness to this very industrial scene at Brighton Power station in 1979. *Troup Head* and sister vessel *Tod Head* sometimes visited with coal cargoes as the older steam colliers were 'thinning out'. Still geared for general trading with high mast platforms, derricks and winches, coal nevertheless continued to be an important coastal commodity at this time. *Tod Head* had traded in associate company Henry & Macgregor's colours, previously.

164. CAERNARVON and LANCING

Entering the eastern Arm at Shoreham in 1971 was Shell's tanker *Caernarvon*, 1,204grt. At this time Shell and B.P. were running individual coastal fleets. *Caernarvon* dated from 1971 and instead of hose derricks had a sophisticated framework boom arrangement for shore connections. Later this ship joined Whitakers coastal fleet as *Whithaven*. Lying over at the coal wharf is the collier *Lancing*, once one of the most regular callers at the old Gas works. *Lancing*, built in 1958 by Austin & Pickersgill, Sunderland, had by this time seen two changes. One, collier 'brown' replaced by white upperworks, and second the ship had been 'jumboised' by the insertion of an extra 20ft mid section, thereby increasing her deadweight by 200 tons to 2,254. In 1978 the ship went to Panamanian flag, and with another of those minimal strokes of the paint brush, became *Landing*.

165. FALKENBERG

Flags of convenience were growing in popularity when this 1980s photograph was taken at the new grain terminal in Portslade. Gone are the incessant visitations of British colliers bringing coal to the Gas works quay. Registered in the Cypriot port of Limassol, the 1971 built 1,587grt. *Falkenberg* looks very well kept, she was fitted with one very large and capable midships crane, definitely not required here for spout loading of grain. Green was another colour in the ascendancy for ships' hulls.

166. ARCO TEST

Another suction dredger, *Arco Test* had started out as *Amey II*, and was well known in the Sussex ports. Although fairly unremarkable, the 594grt 1971 built ship does show an increasing trend - a totally enclosed bridge structure from port to starboard, and curved platework is giving way to more angular, cheaper to fabricate designs. A smooth voyage out to the dredging grounds looks imminent. The photograph dates from 1980.

167. LORA

Once a member of the well known Dutch Carebeka Management fleet, this general cargo ship started as *Carebeka VII*, in 1972. Fully masted and with a good set of cargo derricks she would suit most cargoes on offer. At just under 2,500dwt tons, this was quite a large ship to berth in the River Adur, at Shoreham in 2002. *Lora* has had several names in between, and would appear to have been fortunate to survive 30 years in trade, given the trends. In general terms, by the year 2000, ships with traditional cargo masts and derricks were becoming something of a rarity - it was either no gear at all, or, some kind of crane more likely to be fitted.

168.1 CHICHESTER STAR
This is Littlehampton entrance in about 1978. (See picture 156 for *Chichester City* in 1970)

168.2 BRUNITA
The 1973 built Norweigian *Brunita*, 1,480grt has an advanced cargo handling arrangement, in the form of a 'four-legged' bi-pod mast. The two conventional derricks are rigged in such a way that electric winches control guys, runners and topping lifts, thereby, making for a crane-like operation. By no means fully loaded, the timber stow looking quite gappy, *Brunita* is not down to the marks, as she enters the Prince Philip Lock at Southwick, in 1973.

169. BRIDGEMAN

A 6,000dwt ton clean products tanker, built in 1973, this ship's 1939 namesake predecessor was of 504dwt tons. Seen fully discharged in Southwick Canal in 1979, the crew are taking advantage of the ship's light condition before ballasting, in calm waters, to examine parts not normally visible, using the ship's port life boat - just the thing for the job. It would also be a good time to peer into the bow thruster opening, should the need arise. Whilst Bridgeman's upperworks look smart, judging by the weed levels lower down, a docking job was imminent.

170. SENLAC

British Rail's last purpose built ferry for the combined French service from Newhaven to Dieppe, this 1973 roll-on, roll-off ship is seen entering Newhaven in 1977. The funnel colours still that of the joint operator. *Senlac*, 5090grt still has the look of conventional ferries, but the tonnage reflects the upwards trend. Compared to the thirty or forty year careers of some of the earlier ships, *Senlacs'* departure to Greek waters after a mere 12 years service, highlights the increasing pace of change in the cross-channel services.

171.1 and 171.2
SAND SERIN →

1974 built, the 1,219grt *Sand Serin* is seen discarging at North Quay, Newhaven in 2002. Rail connections to the wharf have gone, and sand, ballast, stone and scrap metal cargoes are in the forefront of operations. Compare this scene with the 'multi-craned' 1961, Durhambrook view.

172. ARCO TYNE

Ships in many categories have increased in size quite dramatically in the search for cost savings and more efficient ways of working. *Arco Tyne* 2,973grt and 4,357dwt was built in 1975 and, in line with another new trend for dredgers, is fitted to self-discharge her cargo of sand or ballast. A single large unit could now do the work of a small fleet from earlier days, the down side of course being preclusion from many of the smaller ports, physically incapable of receiving them. *Arco Tyne's* general layout and appearance is quite conventional, other than the large amount of equipment needed on deck for the self discharging apparatus. Photographed at Shoreham entrance in 2002.

173. KINDRENCE →

The old established fleet of Crescent Shipping as previously seen has operated Thames barges, auxiliaries, motor barges and coasters. In 1976 they took delivery of *Kindrence* and *Luminence*, 1,596grt and 3,210dwt tons respectively. In traditional terms they were colliers, but with the general decline of the coal trade the term mini-bulkers has come to the fore. Both these ships often brought coal to the power station at Shoreham. No doubt very efficiently, as being modern motor ships they would be ideal replacements for the steamers. In the 1977 photograph, *Kindrence* has just entered the Canal, and is about to pass *Schiaffino* en route to the grab cranes. The Crescent red-brown hull looks immaculate on the new ship.

174. VEGAMAN →

Built in 1976 the *Vegaman*, 3,560dwt was a dual purpose clean oil chemical tanker, and one of a series for her owners, Rowbothams. However, at this particular period in that Company's long history they were under the wing of Ingrams, of the U.S.A. and it is their funnel insignia carried by the *Vegaman* seen leaving Shoreham in 1978. *Vegaman's* individual tank venting pipework can be seen grouped in two 'batches' along the catwalk. Later this ship became *Stolt Oakwood*.

← 175.1 WD MEDWAY
Replacing the old harbour bucket dredgers, which needed tug and hopper barges, special suction/hopper dredgers have largely taken over port dredging work. Once the hopper is full of mud, the ship proceeds to the dumping ground offshore. *WD Medway*, 1,962grt of 1976, is seen working off Newhaven breakwater in 1980. (compare with 1933 *Foremost Prince*)

↙ 175.2 THAMES
The 1977 built 677grt Dutch dredger *Thames* is seen at work clearing the main channel at Shoreham in 1980, the suction arm lowered on the starboard side. Periodic dredging is vital to maintain channel depth.

176. ALDR1NGTON
Built by Swan, Hunter at Wallsend, the 4,334grt *Aldrington* is continuing her owners naming of ships after Sussex places. The 1978 photograph shows the ship dressed overall, well, at least forward, on the occasion of her maiden voyage to Shoreham, in part-laden mode. Although of similar length to the old steamers so long in this trade, *Aldrington* is several feet wider and could load to 23ft. draught, if required to carry a full load of 6,500 tons. An 8 cylinder Mirrless Blackstone engine gives a speed of 14kts, an unheard of velocity in steam collier days. White upperworks have well and truly replaced collier 'tan', and 'mini-bulker', in terminology. In 1979, a sister vessel, *Ashington*, came into service.

177. ROMERAL

Spanish container ships *Jaral* and *Romeral* were operating to the Iberian Peninsular and Canary Islands, c.1980. In the 1980 photograph, *Romeral* is arriving at Shoreham with both 20ft and 40ft containers as deck load. These ships, built in 1978, were really gearless cargo ships with extra wide hatches to maximise container stowage. From the visible amount of red boottopping paint, there is no great tonnage of cargo onboard this trip.

178. HEINRICH S.
Naval architects were certainly challenging perceived notions of traditional ship design, when this 4,298grt 3,530dwt ton Roll-on, Roll-off, Lift-on, Lift-off cargo ship appeared in 1979. From a German yard, the bridge structure has migrated right to the bow, the engine room absolutely aft, and an enormous long and wide hatch area is served by two big deck cranes. Where such suitable facilities exist the ship may also be loaded/unloaded via the large stern ramp. All in all, a very versatile ship - since all accommodation is right forward, one could forgive the duty engineer from feeling a little isolated. Photographed in 1980 at Eastern Arm, Shoreham.

179. STENA CAMBRIA

The 12,705grt *Stena Cambria*, the ex *St.Anselm*, closed the Newhaven to Dieppe route in January 1999 after an all too short liason between P&0 and Stena Line, in whose joint colours the ship was painted. This was the last ex railway ship to operate on the crossing and for a while the route remained closed altogether. In the aerial photo the ship looks immaculate. She went out to the Mediterranean for further service, shortly thereafter, just twenty years since construction.

180. LIZZONIA

Another well known coaster operator was J.Wharton of Keadby, the ships in this fleet all having names ending in 'ONIA'. The 1980 built *Lizzonia* 909grt represents the smaller type of 'mini-bulker' coaster, and is adorned in a pale blue colour scheme far removed from collier brown. Coal was still black and dusty but the trade was much in decline when this 1980 photograph was taken; indeed, the old wharf facility itself had but a few years to operate at Southwick. *Lizzonia* later joined F.T.Everard & Sons, as *Capacity*.

181. VOLVOX ANGLIA

1980 built at Papenburg, this 982grt, 1,829dwt trailing suction hopper dredger is seen clearing Shoreham's fairway in 2002. Ships of this sophisticated type have now largely taken over from the 'bucket dredgers', and one particular advantage is the ease at which the channel can be vacated to allow passing traffic. Mooring wires always needed to be slacked down, often frequently in busy spots and duly winch tensioned again before dredging could resume, with the older type. From the bow pipe arrangement, *Volvox Anglia* would be capable of land reclamation work, by pumping dredgings ashore, if required.

182.1 SHEVRELL ↗

James Tyrrell Ltd of Ireland had run coasters for many years, becoming part of Arklow Shipping Ltd. Their smart 1981 built mini bulker *Shevrell*, 1,981grt has just entered Southwick's Prince Philip Lock, in 1985. Note the ornate bow crest, not much seen in modern times. *Shevrell* went to Cyprus in 1998, as *Garibaldi*.

182.2 HARTING →

Wallsend built by Clellands in 1981, the 1,584grt *Harting* continues her owners trend of Sussex place naming. With two very long hatchways where in earlier years three or four would have featured, mineral cargoes other than coal would be frequent by the time of this 1990 photograph.

183. DIEPPE (5)

Photographed in 2002 and looking resplendent in her new Transmanche livery, although devoid of sheer and rather box-like, this 1981 built ferry is at, 17,672grt, unquestionably the largest roll-on, roll-off type yet seen at Newhaven. With the new century has come another new operator in the form of Transmanche Ferries of Dieppe. Fitted with bow visor and twin stern ramps, *Dieppe* should certainly be able to cope with some traffic. She started life in the Baltic area as *Saga Star*, and at 479ft (146m), by 78ft (24m) is larger than the ocean trading cargo ships that visited Newhaven previously. It is interesting to compare relative ship sizes on the route over the 150 years - *Dieppe* has been a popular name:

Year built					
1847	SS	*Dieppe* (1)	263grt.	153ft.6in.	(46.7m)
1853	SS	*Dieppe* (2)	360 "	181ft.6in.	(55 3m)
1875	SS	*Dieppe* (3)	432 " (cargo)	168ft.5in.	(51.3m)
1905	SS	*Dieppe* (4)	1,215 "	274ft.	(83.5m)
1930	SS	*Worthing*	2,294 "	306ft.	(93.3m)
1973	MV	*Senlac*	5,590 "	390ft.	(118.9m)
1980	MV	*Stena Cambria*	12,705 "	423ft.	(128.9m)
1981	MV	*Dieppe* (5)	17,672 "	479ft.	(146m)

This large increase in ship size is even more noticeable on routes elsewhere. Ferries commonly measure 20-30,000grt and 50,000 tonners are imminent - larger than most ocean liners in the pre-jet plane era, but that's another story.

184. MERIDIAN II

Astern and up-river of the *Chichester City* at Kingston Wharves on the River Adur lie two similar tonnaged craft, yet they present totally different profiles. Centre lies the 1,499grt *Meridian II*, a type of cargo vessel rapidly growing in popularity in the 1980s. She is a L.A.D. 'low air draught' vessel, specially designed to trade anywhere around Europe but with the ability to voyage far into Europes' great river systems. The whole wheelhouse support structure can be lowered down into the hull, this is in the form of a large square steel section, and carries all the cabling for the navigation and control of the ship. Masts are hinged, so that minimum air draught whether loaded or in ballast can be achieved, yet with the wheelhouse fully raised, cargo can still be stowed on top of the hatch covers. The Captain and Officers access the bridge by way of steel side ladders which slide back in trackways, as the whole is lowered. Astern of the 1982 built *Meridian II* a more conventional form of cargo ship is moored; this ship has two tracked deck cranes to work cargo. *Bellatrix* and *Meridian II* are both lifting scrap in the 1990 scene.

185. HOO VENTURE

The growth and success of R.Lapthorn's coasting fleet in the last two decades has been a rare success story for the British Flag. Lapthorn's have built up a fleet of about two dozen very efficient 'mini-bulkers' in three or four size categories, and very few ports still commercially active are not visited by them. *Hoo Venture*, 498grt and 1,236dwt, represents the smallest class. Built by the Yorkshire Drydock Company, Hull, two oil engines and twin screws provide the power and manoeuvrability. Yorkshire Drydock had a long and successful production run for this type of coaster, building for a number of owners. In the 2002 photograph, *Hoo Venture* is seen arriving at Cowes, I.O.W., and the recent fitting of an hydraulic excavator type crane is another growing trend with coastal shipping. Once again coasters are becoming 'geared' for self discharging or loading. The capacity of excavators can be enormous, enabling the ship to discharge in a few hours - very efficiently and economically. *Hoo Venture* was built in 1982.

186.1 and 186.2
SEA KITE ↗

The 1983 built *Sea Kite*, 1,785grt, had originally been named *Cowdray*, then *Ballygrainey*. By 2001, she was being operated under the Barbados flag by Torbulk. Compare this scene to the *SS Arundel* (1970) view, amazingly the only real constants are the foreground and the English Channel, beyond.

← 187.1 HANNY TRADER

1984 constructed, 1,289grt and 1,536dwt, this green hulled LAD coaster previously operated as *Sea Tyne*. Similar in configuration to *Meridian II*, the folding masts and sliding side ladders to the retractable wheelhouse, can be clearly seen. However, the crew need not fret, Newhaven's swingbridge is about to open, up ahead. The 2002 photo shows the ship in dire need of deweeding, or speed will soon be much reduced. The ferry *Dieppe* lies beyond, at the loading ramp.

↙ 187.2 MASTIFF & RINGACOLTIG

As *Hanny Trader* passes by, the ex-Navy tug *Mastiff*, 1968, 152t, lies alongside the grab dredger *Ringacoltig*, awaiting action. *Ringacoltig* 434grt was built and owned at Cork, Ireland in 1974.

188. TRAVEMAR AFRICA

Built in Spain and registered in Valencia in 1984, this very solidly constructed ship is seen departing Shoreham in 1986, the harbour tug *Adurni*, on the bow line. At 5,717grt and 9,300dwt *Travemar Africa* had brought in a part cargo of logs. With three large hatches served by deck cranes, she would be capable of trading anywhere worldwide. A stern mooring anchor is not such a common feature. In 1991, *Travemar Africa* was sold, becoming *Maritsa NP*.

189. BOE SEA

A number of heavily geared ships worked in the log trade from West Africa, where ship's equipment had to be able to lift the logs aboard. *Boe Sea*, Panamanian flag and of Japanese build in 1985, was a typical example at 5,451grt and 8,800dwt tons. The goalpost masts are very substantial indeed, and rigged as we have seen before in such a way that the large conventional derricks operate as if they were crane booms. Topping lifts are doubled via electric winches, meaning the derricks do not need to be guyed, at deck level. The photograph is c.1988.

190. ANNE BOYE & KARIN

The Danish Shipowner H.C.Boye specialises in traditionally geared cargo ships of modest tonnage. These ships are able to trade to remote small ports and islands with little infrastructure, and may discharge to lighters overside. *Anne Boye*, 1,501grt and built in 1985, is fitted with very conventional cargo gear - quite a rarity by the end of the 20th century. Astern of the *Anne Boye*, the German cargo vessel *Karin*, is almost hiding behind her own vast raised hatch covers- one can only hope they are never opened fully at sea. *Karin*, of 1,986grt, is an excellent example of just how far ship design and profiles have come, compare to 1930, *SS Vard*, of the same tonnage. The brand new gas fired power station presides over all, yet will never require an entire fleet of ships to sustain it. The scene was photographed in 2002 at Southwick.

191. HMS ARUN

Seen leaving Shoreham in 1987 is *HMS Arun*, one of the Royal Navy's new minesweepers of 640 dwt tons. This vessel was built at Lowestoft.

192.1 and 192.2 TRITON →

Beck's of Groningen, in the Netherlands have operated coasters for many a year. *Triton*, at 999grt, 1,544dwt, smartly kept, is now one of the smallest in her owner's fleet. In the first photograph, the 1986 built ship has just discharged a stone cargo at Rye Harbour Wharf, where her shallow draught would be well suited to the Rother channel. In the second scene, also in the year 2002, *Triton* has just left Cowes and is proceeding down the Western Solent towards the Needles.

193. HOO MAPLE

The 1989 constructed *Hoo Maple* is the next larger size in her owner's fleet. At 794grt and 1,399dwt the Lapthorn ship is seen at the old railway wharf in Littlehampton in 2002. Using her own deck mounted excavator the ship has just unloaded a stone cargo to the quayside, the hatches closed, excavator placed into its seagoing position, all that is now required will be the incoming tide, for the off. Note the last shore crane has gone but the gasometer remains just as colourful as ever. Compare this to the 1946 *Suavity* scene (1970), again the change in ship form is considerable. In the *Hoo Maple* photo the wharf has been totally reconstructed with steel facing piles, and the days when British Railway's smallest type of steam shunting engine was allowed on the wharf, are long gone.

194. ARCO DART

Pictured here just above Newhaven's swingbridge in 2002 is the direct successor to the *Pen Dart*, already described. *Arco Dart* was built in 1990 together with a sister ship, *Arco Dee*. The 1,309grt suction dredgers are in design terms some light years away from the earlier types. The suction pipes can clearly be seen along the starboard side, whilst most of the remaining apparatus pertains to the self-discharging ability, by conveyor belt to the quayside. *Arco Dart* is of the bridge and accommodation in the bow type, this presumably affording some maindeck weather protection when dredging. Compare with the 1957 built *Pen Dart*. Familiar in the Sussex ports, this class is now their owner's smallest.

← 195.1 and 195.2
CITY OF CHICHESTER

Another direct 'descendant' from an earlier fleet, this 1997 Devon built, 2,046grt vessel can lift 2,800 tons at full draught. Of very wide beam she can, nevertheless, berth at Littlehampton, her port of Registry. At 72m x 15m x 5.2m and with substantial self-discharging gear - a steady stream of sand or ballast may be deposited on the quayside, by way of travelling gantry crane and grab, hopper, conveyor belts and a long discharging 'arm'. In these 2003 photographs an interesting comparison can be made with the locally owned *Pen Adur* see No.74, and *Chichester City* see No.156.

196. SUPERSEACAT ONE

A very far cry indeed from conventional ferries, this 4,700grt vessel can, by virtue of her design run at 38 knots. The hull is of the 'high speed monohull' configuration and as such the Italian built, Hoverspeed operated *Superseacat One* is able to sail in most conditions. Some of the true catamaran types have less of a heavy weather ability, whereas the traditional cross channel ferries just 'ploughed on'. *Superseacat One* handles the busier summer traffic of passengers and cars, on the Newhaven to Dieppe route. The 2002 photograph gives a clear indication of manoeuvrability, as she enters Newhaven stern first towards the berth. Below the 'leaping feline' motif can be seen the warning symbol '⊗' for the bow thruster. One of several similar vessels *Superseacat One* was built in 1997.

← 197. NIKAR G

As if to highlight Shipowners' increasing liking for blue hulls, *Nikar G* is seen leaving Shoreham in 2002. Antiguan flagged and built by Daewoo in Korea, this 2,335grt ship is of the high hatchway type. The individual hatch cover slabs are removed by way of a travelling gantry on track arrangement, and placed at each end in a stack until re-closing is required. Masts are 'minimalist' and the accommodation arrangements reflect the small number of crew required to run such ships, nowadays. Another age old institution has evolved whereby port and starboard lifeboats may be replaced with a single aft fitted gravity type on a track; or, a rescue boat for emergencies, plus of course the statutory life rafts. *Nikar G* also has bow thruster assistance for manoeuvring. The ship was completed in 2000.

← 198. RIVER ALN

SCS BULK operate this 2,858grt 4,850dwt ton mini-bulker seen here discharging at Southwick in 2002. A shore based excavator is unloading a mineral cargo, and the ship's hatch cover slabs can be seen stacked at each end of the hold area, again positioned by tracked gantry gear. The flag of Antigua flies at the stern. This class of vessel has a traditional height bridge structure enabling containers to be stacked on deck, should trade require. As this is the last vessel described herein, it is pleasing to note that we are now in the third century whereby the black, silver banded funnel has been evident in a Sussex port.

199. Arundel 2002

With the Castle as ever standing guard above, the smart properties on the north bank of the River Arun stand in great contrast to the activities hereabouts, one hundred years ago. Along the grassy bank on the right hand side once stood small docks cut in, where barges and small craft worked cargo. Barges took various materials inland above Arundel Bridge, to Bury, Stopham, Fittleworth, Pulborough, Petworth and Midhurst etc, as well as to connect with the Wey and Arun Navigation in pre railway days. The Arun barges could set a small spritsail and aided with the current and the use of stout poles, could get along with up to about 40 tons cargo, at best. The town side bank had been the site of T.Isemonger's shipyard in the mid 1800's, building brigs and various sailing coastal types. It has been a long time since a steam tug's whistle heralded the arrival of a coal brig. See *Ebernezer* and *Jumna* for similar location scenes.

200.1 and 200.2 Littlehampton 2002

This is the seawards view from the retractable footbridge at Littlehampton on the site of the old swingbridge. Yachts and fishing boats now predominate at moorings where the shipwrights of Harveys turned out so many sea going commercial craft up to pre World War I in their Clymping Yard. On the east or town bank, smart homes have appeared where once the timber barquentines and latterly, the dredgers discharged their cargoes. The large distant crane indicates further building work is imminent. However, at least we enter the 21st. century with all four Sussex ports described, still visited by commercial shipping, unlike many of the Country's smaller harbours.

200.3 Littlehampton 2003

Spanning the River Arun into the new millenium is the arc of the foot/cycle bridge. Making an interesting comparison with its 1908 forbear and indeed, the old chain ferry. The bridge simply withdraws into a tracked recess on the west bank, when in opening mode for the passage of high masted craft. Another change- the Bridgeman's operating 'eyrie' has moved from mid-stream. Heavy road traffic can now cross unhindered some way up stream, by new road bridge. (see 34 for similar views.) In the third photograph the retractable footbridge over the Arun is already into closing mode, astern of City of Chichester. With her self-discharging arm now stowed for the sea passage, the cargo unloaded at Littlehampton can just be made out on the quayside distant. Behind the ship, on the Clymping bank those fine sailing ships had been produced earlier, and yachts in abundance. The 2003 photo location on a new riverside walk now sports smart riverside apartments; a far cry from the once industrial heart of the port.

201.1 and 201.2 Lewes 2002

The view downstream from Cliffe Bridge, once the scene of so much seagoing activity, is surprisingly little altered. Warehouses and riverside factories have become very fashionable. Compare to 1893 *Jachin* (c.1900) for the same view. Upstream, mercifully, something traditional continues - and long may it so prosper.

202.1 and 202.2 Asham Quay, River Ouse 2003

Still looking neat and tidy despite the intervening 36 years since the departure of the last shipboard cargo of cement downriver, the old concrete crane rail mounts survive. Just over the low backwall some evidence remains of ironwork relating to the river end of the aerial pylon ropeway which ran across the fields bringing the cement bags to the wharf. This idyllic remote location was surely unique, being about one mile upriver from Southease Swing Bridge and Railway Halt, yet not road connected at all. (see 27.1, 27.2 and *Celtic* photographs in particular for comparison)

203. Southease Swing Bridge 2003

Built in the 1880s, the manually operated bridge had to be opened for shipping proceeding upriver to Lewes, Southerham quay and finally Asham until 1967. Today the single tracked bridge forms a vital cross river link for walkers along the South Downs Way, and a means of local access for the nearby farms. This point is about 4½ miles from the sea at Newhaven and the heavy duty piling which once fended off ships from the bridge supports is still very much in situ. Although low tide when the photograph was taken it is easy to see how 250 ton ships drawing between 8ft and 10ft, could make their way up to Asham, given a decent rise of tide.

204. Piddinghoe 2003
In the delightful village of Piddinghoe, 3½ miles from the sea, lay Every's Wharf, just across from the Church. This facility was built about 100 years ago in order to accept larger cargoes for the Phoenix Ironworks at Lewes than could reach that place directly. Initially goods were transhipped onward by barge, but as with most things, motor lorry transport won the day. Little used after the Second World War, except for a few scrap metal cargoes, private dwellings now stand where the last coasters called in the early 1950s. (see picture 10 - *Alert*)

← 205.1 and 205.2 Rye Harbour Entrance 2003

As in centuries past work continues to hold back the eternal litoral shingle drift at this location, otherwise the harbour mouth would soon deviate and block. Seen entering on the top of the tide is *Hoocreek* 671grt and on her way to Rye Harbour Wharf. This is the second ship of the name, the earlier version being an ex Dutch coaster of 209 tons built in 1928. *Hoocreek*, unlike her 1982 sister *Hoo Venture* (see 185), has not been fitted with cargo gear. In the lower picture Rye Harbour Village is just visible about a mile ahead up the straight Rother Channel. Rye Harbour Nature Reserve is to the left of the trackway - another splendid Sussex spot.

206. Rye from the South West 2003

This scene directly relates to No. 36 *Gwynhelen*, although, now populated by yachts. The River Brede emerges from a lock bottom left to join the Tillingham. Tight bends have always constrained the size of craft able to percolate as far as Strand Quay. Mercifully, the Rye skyline has not much altered in the last seventy years or so.

207.1 and 207.2 RYE STRAND QUAY 2003

With the domination of leisure and pleasure craft, the ancient Strand Quay, once the scene of much cargo loading and unloading, is now a favourite visitor attraction. By boat the sea is the best part of three miles away or two and a half as the crow flies. For comparison views see 14, 23 37, 145, & 160 from earlier shipping days.

Bibliography

The Story of Shoreham	Henry Cheal	1923	
Mercantile Navy List		1934	
A History of the Southern Railway	C.F:Dendy Marshall	1936	
Merchant Ships 1949-50	E.C.Talbot Booth	1950	
A Handbook of Sailing Barges	F. S. Cooper and		
	John Chancellor	1955	
The Worlds Tankers	Laurence Dunn	1956	
Merchant Ships 1963	F.C.Talbot Booth	1963	
Modern Ships	R.Carpenter DSC	1970	
Down Tops'l	H.Benham	1971	0 245506 61 6
South Eastern Sail	Michael Bouquet	1972	0 715355 92 9
Steam Coasters & Short Sea Traders	Charles V. Waine	1976	0 905184 04 1
A Maritime History of Rye	John Collard	1978	0 950627 62 3
Victorian & Edwardian Ships & Harbours	Basil Creenhill and		
	Ann Giffard	1978	0 713410 79 5
Sailormen between the Wars	John Allendale	1978	
Paddle Steamers	Bernard Cox	1979	0 713702 94 3
Stephenson, Clarke Shipping	Craig J.M.Carter	1981	0 905617 17 7
British Steam Tugs	P.N.Thomas	1983	0 905184 07 6
Brighton to Worthing	Vic Mitchell and		
	Keith Smith	1983	0 906520 03 7
Gas & Electricity Colliers	D.Ridley Chesterton		
	R.S.Fenton	1984	0 905617 33 9
West Sussex Waterways	P.A.L.Vine	1985	0 906520 24 X
Coasters,Schepen van der Kustvaart	A.Boerma	1985	9 060139 28 3
Kent & East Sussex Waterways	P.A.L.Vine	1989	0 906520 72 X
The Steam Collier Fleets	J.A.Macrae and		
	C.V.Waine	1990	0 905184 12 2
Lower Ouse Navigation	Alan F. Hill	1991	
Carebeka 1939-1983	J.H.Anderiesse		
	E.A.Kruidhof		
	J.Oostmeijer	1995	0 905617 78 9
Maritime Sussex	David Harries	1997	1 857701 22 4
Ferry Services of the			
London, Brighton and South Coast Railway	S.Jordan	1998	0 853615 21 7

Lloyds Registers/Publications
Sea Breezes Magazines (early)
Ships Illustrated Magazines

Local Newspapers
World Ship Society- Marine News

List of Illustrations

28	Newhaven Swingbridge	(c1920)	79.1	SS KEYNES	1946
29	SS BRENTWOOD	1904	79.2	SS KEYNES at Newhaven	(c1950
30	SS DIEPPE	1905	80	SS LONDONBROOK	1946
31	Portslade Gas Works	(c1905)	81	MV SUAVITY	1946
32.1	Southwick Lock	(c1905)	82	SS ALEXANDROS X	1946
32.2	Southwick Lock & Canal	(c1905)	83	PS WAVERLEY	1947
33	SEASTONE	1907	84	MV RENNES	1947
34.1	Littlehampton Crossing	(c1906)	85	SS FALAISE	1947
34.2	Littlehampton Swing Bridge	(1908)	86.1	SS BRANKSOME	1948
34.3	Littlehampton chain ferry	(1908)	86.2	MV BROADHURST	1948
35	CLYMPING	1909	87	SS LUGANO	1949
36.1	ANNA	1909	88.1	MV COMITY	1949
36.2	GWYNHELEN	1909	88.2	MV AGNES	1949
37.1	Rye from the South	(c1910)	89.1	SS MAID OF ORLEANS	1949
37.2	Strand Quay	(c1910)	89.2	SS BRIGHTON	1950
38.1	SS ROUEN	1911	90	SS CLIFF QUAY	1950
38.2	Sheerlegs/SS WALBROOK	1910	91	MV DAME CAROLINE HASLETT	1950
39.1	SS SEABORNE ALPHA	1912	92	MV BATTERSEA	1951
39.2	SS MUNGRET	1912	93.1	MV TOTLAND	1952
40	ST ADUR II	1912	93.2	MV ZAANSTROOM	1952
41	SS J.B.PADDON	1917	94.1	SS LORD WARDEN	1952
41	PT STELLA	1879	94.2	SS LISIEUX	1952
42	SS AGHIOS GIORGIOS II	1916	95.1	MT KITE	1952
43	REINA II	1910	95.2	HMS FITTLETON	1953
44	MOULTONIAN	1919	96.1	MV GLENSHIRA (as cargo)	1953
45.1	Scandinavian timber ships		96.2	MV GLENSHIRA (salvage)	(1980)
	at Littlehampton	(1920)	97	SS SIR WILLIAM WALKER	1954
45.2	FLORA	1919	98	MV GEORGE BOWER	1954
45.3	CHRISTENSEN	1920	98	MV JAN HAMM	1954
46	Steam coaster, Littlehampton	(c1930)	99	SS JAMES ROWAN	1955
47	SS REX	1919	100	SS JAN TURTLEJSKI	1955
48	Sunset, Aldrington B.	(c1918)	101	M DURHAMBROOK	1955
49	The Mystery Tower	(c1920)	102.1	SS ZAPADNAJA DVINA	1955
50	SS JELLICOE ROSE	1920	102.2	SS ZAPADNAJA " (midships view)	(1975)
51	SS DONA FLORA	1924	103.1	MV SHELL WELDER	1955
52	FOREMOST 22	1924	103.2	SS ADUR	1955
53	WILL EVERARD	1925	104	MV WINSTON	1955
54	SS PASS OF MELFORT	1926	105	MV WERA	1955
55	MT CALDERGATE	1927	106	SS ARUNDEL	1956
56	PS SUSSEX QUEEN	1927	107.1	MVs PICONEGRO	1956
57	MV FERROCRETE	1927		PICOGRIS	1957
58	SS WORTHING	1928		PICOMAR	1953
59	MV ANNA	1929	107.2	PICONEGRO (painting)	(1967)
60	Ford Railway Bridge	(1929)	108.1	MV IVY B	1956
61.1	SS LA PLATA	1930	108.2	MV IVY B (drydock)	(1980)
61.2	SS VARD	1930	109.	MV BUENOS AIRES STAR	1956
62	MV MEDINA	1931	110.1	MV KIRTONDYKE	1957
63	MT TILLERMAN	1931	110.2	MV BRANDON	1957
64	SS FOREMOST PRINCE	1933	111.	MV BELGIA	1957
65.1	SS PETWORTH	1934	112	MV BERND GUNDA	1957
65.2	SS OLAV ASBJØRN	1934	113.1	MV WALTER RICHTER	1957
66	MT BEN OLIVER	1935	113.2	MV WATERDALE	(c1973
67	SS LECONFIELD	1935	114.1	MV ARABRITT	1957
68	MV SAND MARTIN	1936	114.2	MV PEN DART	1957
69	SS ARTHUR WRIGHT	1937	115	MV CON ZELO	1957
70	PS RYDE	1937	116	MV HERON	1957
71	MV DRAKE	1937	117	MV HUMPHREY GILBERT	1957
72	TSS EMPRESS QUEEN	1940	118	MV AMETHYST/FAITH	1958
73	SS ESSO TIOGA	1943	119	MV QUEENSLAND	1958
74	MV PEN ADUR	1943	120	MT PETWORTH	1958
75.1	MV SAND SKIPPER	1943	121	MV RON WOOLAWAY	1958
75.2	MT OCLEAN PULLER	1943	122	MV STORRINGTON	1959
76	ST CHRIANIE	1944	123	MV SHEKNALES	1964
77.1	SS LEVENWOOD	1945	123	MV SAND GULL	1959
77.2	ST B.P.MANAGER	1945	124.1	MV HUMBER LEE	1959
78	SS OLIVER BURY	1946	124.2	RYE TRADER	1959

125	MV ROYA	1959	168.2	BRUNITA	1973
126.1	MV DORSET COAST	1959	169	BRIDGEMAN	1973
126.2	MT ESSO IPSWICH	1960	170	SENLAC	1973
127.1	MT MEECHING	1960	171.1	SAND SERIN	1974
127.2	MT MEECHING at Southwick	(c1978)	171.2	SAND SERIN at Newhaven	(2003)
128.1	MT KINGSTON BUCI	1960	172	ARCO TYNE	1975
128.2	MT KINGSTOON BUCI ship handling	(c1970)	173	KINDRENCE	1976
129	SS HARDWICKE GRANGE	1961	174	VEGAMAN	1976
130	MV DESEADO	1961	175.1	WD MEDWAY	1976
131.1	MT ESSO DOVER	1961	175.2	THAMES	1977
131.2	MT ESSO JERSEY	1962	176	ALDRINGTON	1978
132	MV ANN M	1962	177	ROMERAL	1978
133.1	MV ATHENE	1962	178	HEINRICH S	1979
133.2	MV ERNA OLDENDORFF	1962	179	STENA CAMBRIA	1980
134	MV FORT CREVECOEUR	1962	180	LIZZONIA	1980
135	MV MAGUELONE	1963	181	VOLVOX ANGLIA	1980
136	MV SW2	1963	182.1	SHEVRELL	1981
137	MV DICTION	1963	182.2	HARTING	1981
138	FRIVOLITY	1963	183	DIEPPE (5)	1981
139	RRS JOHN MURRAY	1963	184	MERIDIAN II	1982
140.1	MT BOLTON	1964	185	HOO VENTURE	1982
140.2	MT HAMBLE	1964	186.1	SEA KITE	1983
141	MV CAPELLA	1965	186.2	SEA KITE at Southwick Canal	(2002)
142	MV FRIGG	1965	187.1	HANNY TRADER	1984
143	MV RYNSTROOM	1965	187.2	MASTIFF	1968
144.1	MV GABROVO	1965		RINGACOLTIG	1974
144.2	MV JEMRIX	1965		(both at Newhaven)	(2003)
145	MV EDWARD STONE	1965	188	TRAVEMAR AFRICA	1984
146	MV VALENCAY	1965	189	BOE SEA	1985
147	MV FREE ENTERPRISE II	1965	190	ANNE BOYE	1985
148	MT BEECHCROFT	1966	190	KARIN	1985
149	MV PERSEY III	1968	191	HMS ARUN (photograph)	(1987)
150	MV YANTARNYI	1968	192.1	TRITON	1986
Prefix dropped hereafter			192.2	TRITON leaving Cowes	(2002)
151	ATHINA B	1968	193	HOO MAPLE	1989
152.1	ACCLIVITY	1968	194	ARCO DART	1990
153.1	LEADSMAN	1968	195.1	CITY OF CHICHESTER	1997
153.2	EURCO FAITH	1968	195.2	” at Littlehampton	(2003)
154	DESTEL	1969	196	SUPERSEACAT ONE	1997
155	SAND SWIFT	1969	197	NIKAR G	2000
156	CHICHESTER CITY	1970	198	RIVER ALN	2001
157	JUNIOR	1970	199	Arundel waterfront	(2002)
158	ULIDIA	1970	200.1	Littlehampton, west bank	(2002)
159	EXXTOR I	1970	200.2	Littlehampton footbridge	(2003)
160	Rye, Strand Quay	(c1970)	200.3	Littlehampton footbridge open	(2003)
161	SCHIAFFINO	1970	201.1	Lewes, downstream	(2002)
162.	Royal Sovereign Light Tower	(1970)	201.2	Lewes, upstream	(2002)
163	TROUP HEAD	1971	203	Southease swingbridge	(2003)
164	CAERNARVON	1971	204	Piddinghoe	(2003)
164	LANCING	1958	205.1	Rye Harbour entrance	(2003)
165	FALKENBERG	1971	205.2	Rye Rother Channel	(2003)
166	ARCO TEST	1971	206	Rye from the Southwest	(2003)
167	LORA	1972	207.1	Rye Strand Quay (S)	(2003)
168.1	CHICHESTER STAR	1973	207.2	Rye Strand Quay (N)	(2003)

Index

PORTSMOUTH	26.1	SAND SKIPPER	75.1	TILLERMAN	63
QUEENSLAND	119	SAND SWIFT	155	TOD HEAD	163
		SARAH	3	TOTLAND	93.1
REINA II	43	SCHIAFFINO	161	TRAVEMAR AFRICA	188
RENNES	84	SEA KITE	186.1	TRITON	192.1
RESULT	17	SEABORNE ALPHA	39.1	TROUP HEAD	163
REX	47	SEASTONE	33		
RINGACOLTIG	187.2	SENLAC	170	ULIDIA	158
RIVER ALN	198	SHEKSNALES	123		
ROMERAL	177	SHELL WELDER	103.1	VALENCAY	146
RON WOOLAWAY	121	SHEVRELL	182.1	VARD	61.2
ROSIE	12	SIR Wm. WALKER	97	VEGAMA	174
Rother, River (E)	map 5	SISSIE	7	VOLVOX ANGLIA	181
ROUEN	38.1	SIX SISTERS	25		
ROYA	125	SOUTHAMPTON	1	WD MEDWAY	175.1
Royal Sovereign Lt.	162	Southease Bridge	203	WALBROOK	38.2
RYDE	70	Southease Canal	186.2	WALTER RICHTER	113.1
Rye Harbour	88.2	Southwick Lock	32.1	WATERDALE	113.2
Rye Rock Channel	37.1	STELLA	7/41	WAVERLEY	83
Rye Strand Quay	207.1	STENA CAMBRIA	179	WERA	105
RYE TRADER	124.2	STORRINGTON	122	WILL EVERARD	53
RYNSTROOM	143	SUAVITY	81	WINSTON	104
		SUPERSEACAT ONE	196	WORTHING	58
SW2	136	SUSSEX MAID	1	WORTHING BELLE	11.1
SAND GULL	123	SUSSEX QUEEN	56	YANTARNYI	150
SAND MARTIN	68				
SAND SERIN	171.1	THAMES	175.2	ZAANSTROOM	93.2

Acknowledgements

I would like hereby to record thanks and appreciation to all the kind individuals, Societies and Organisations who have so helped in the compilation of this book, with their time, information and material:

The Members of the Committee of the Arundel Museum Society, Brighton Local Studies Library, Cowes Maritime Museum Library, Littlehampton Museum, Newhaven Local and Maritime Museum, Ordnance Survey Office, Rye Castle Museum, Rye Heritage Centre, Skyfotos, Southampton City Council Library, Sussex Archaeological Society, The Argus (Brighton), The World Ship Society. Peter Bailey, Michael Bartlett, Cliff Bloomfield, Allan Downend, Esme Evans, Rebecca Fardell, Susan Hill, Robert Jeeves, Robert Lamb, Norman Langridge, Derdriu McLaughlin, Phil Newman, Tori Parr, Tony Smith and David Whiteside.

Photograph sources:	(Author's collection un-numbered)
Arundel Museum	2, 8
Littlehampton Museum	44
Newhaven Museum	4, 10.1-3, 19, 26.2, 27.2, 57, 79.2
Rye Castle Museum	5, 23, 145
Robert Jeeves Collection	1, 7, 41
Skyfotos	24, 47, 53, 54, 55, 56, 58, 59, 63, 66, 75.1, 88.1, 113.2, 124.2, 138, 179
Sussex Archaeological Society	16
The Argus (Brighton)	27.3, 80, 101
The World Ship Society, Photo Library	13.1, 17, 27.1, 39.1, 50, 51, 65.1, 69, 73, 77.1, 86.1

7 A.E.Banks, 12 Thomas Hibberd James, 13 Reeves collection, 35 F.W.Spry, 36 J.Foster, 39.2 J.White, 41 A.E.Banks, 39.2, 45.1-3 J.White, 48 H.W.Fubbs.

MP Middleton Press

Easebourne Lane, Midhurst, W Sussex. GU29 9AZ Tel: 01730 813169 Fax: 01730 812601

Email: sales@middletonpress.co.uk www.middletonpress.co.uk

If books are not available from your local transport stockist, order direct post free UK.

BRANCH LINES

Branch Line to Allhallows
Branch Line to Alton
Branch Lines around Ascot
Branch Line to Ashburton
Branch Lines around Bodmin
Branch Line to Bude
Branch Lines around Canterbury
Branch Lines around Chard & Yeovil
Branch Lines to Cheddar
Branch Lines around Cromer
Branch Line to the Derwent Valley
Branch Lines to East Grinstead
Branch Lines of East London
Branch Lines to Effingham Junction
Branch Lines around Exmouth
Branch Lines to Falmouth, Helston & St. Ives
Branch Line to Fairford
Branch Lines to Felixstow & Aldeburgh
Branch Lines around Gosport
Branch Line to Hayling
Branch Lines to Henley, Windsor & Marlow
Branch Line to Hawkhurst
Branch Line to Horsham
Branch Lines around Huntingdon
Branch Line to Ilfracombe
Branch Line to Kingsbridge
Branch Line to Kingswear
Branch Line to Lambourn
Branch Lines to Launceston & Princetown
Branch Lines to Longmoor
Branch Line to Looe
Branch Line to Lyme Regis
Branch Line to Lynton
Branch Lines around March
Branch Lines around Midhurst
Branch Line to Minehead
Branch Line to Moretonhampstead
Branch Lines to Newport (IOW)
Branch Lines to Newquay
Branch Lines around North Woolwich
Branch Line to Padstow
Branch Lines to Princes Risborough
Branch Lines to Seaton and Sidmouth
Branch Lines around Sheerness
Branch Line to Shrewsbury
Branch Line to Tenterden
Branch Lines around Tiverton
Branch Line to Torrington
Branch Lines to Tunbridge Wells
Branch Line to Upwell
Branch Line to Wantage
Branch Lines of West London
Branch Lines of West Wiltshire
Branch Lines around Weymouth
Branch Lines around Wimborne
Branch Lines around Wisbech

NARROW GAUGE

Austrian Narrow Gauge
Branch Line to Lynton
Branch Lines around Portmadoc 1923-46
Branch Lines around Porthmadog 1954-94
Branch Line to Southwold
Douglas to Port Erin
Douglas to Peel
Kent Narrow Gauge
Northern France Narrow Gauge
Romneyrail
Southern France Narrow Gauge
Sussex Narrow Gauge
Surrey Narrow Gauge
Swiss Narrow Gauge
Vivarais Narrow Gauge

SOUTH COAST RAILWAYS

Ashford to Dover
Bournemouth to Weymouth
Brighton to Worthing
Dover to Ramsgate
Eastbourne to Hastings
Portsmouth to Southampton
Ryde to Ventnor
Southampton to Bournemouth

SOUTHERN MAIN LINES

Basingstoke to Salisbury
Crawley to Littlehampton
Dartford to Sittingbourne
East Croydon to Three Bridges
Epsom to Horsham
Exeter to Barnstaple
Exeter to Tavistock
London Bridge to East Croydon
Orpington to Tonbridge
Tonbridge to Hastings
Salisbury to Yeovil
Sittingbourne to Ramsgate
Swanley to Ashford
Tavistock to Plymouth
Three Bridges to Brighton
Victoria to Bromley South
Victoria to East Croydon
Waterloo to Windsor
Waterloo to Woking
Woking to Portsmouth
Woking to Southampton
Yeovil to Exeter

EASTERN MAIN LINES

Barking to Southend
Ely to Kings Lynn
Ely to Norwich
Fenchurch Street to Barking
Hitchin to Peterborough
Ilford to Shenfield
Ipswich to Saxmundham
Liverpool Street to Ilford
Saxmundham to Yarmouth
Tilbury Loop

WESTERN MAIN LINES

Bristol to Taunton
Didcot to Banbury
Didcot to Swindon
Ealing to Slough
Exeter to Newton Abbot
Newton Abbot to Plymouth
Newbury to Westbury
Moreton-in-Marsh to Worcester
Oxford to Moreton-in-Marsh
Paddington to Ealing
Paddington to Princes Risborough
Plymouth to St. Austell
Princes Risborough to Banbury
Reading to Didcot
Slough to Newbury
St. Austell to Penzance
Swindon to Bristol
Taunton to Exeter
Westbury to Taunton

MIDLAND MAIN LINES

St. Albans to Bedford
Euston to Harrow & Wealdstone
Harrow to Watford
St. Pancras to St. Albans

COUNTRY RAILWAY ROUTES

Abergavenny to Merthyr
Andover to Southampton
Bath to Evercreech Junction
Bath Green Park to Bristol
Bournemouth to Evercreech Junction
Brecon to Newport
Burnham to Evercreech Junction
Cheltenham to Andover
Croydon to East Grinstead
Didcot to Winchester
East Kent Light Railway
Frome to Bristol
Guildford to Redhill
Reading to Basingstoke
Reading to Guildford
Redhill to Ashford
Salisbury to Westbury
Stratford upon Avon to Cheltenham
Strood to Paddock Wood
Taunton to Barnstaple
Wenford Bridge to Fowey
Westbury to Bath
Woking to Alton
Yeovil to Dorchester

GREAT RAILWAY ERAS

Ashford from Steam to Eurostar
Clapham Junction 50 years of change
Festiniog in the Fifties
Festiniog in the Sixties
Festiniog 50 years of enterprise
Isle of Wight Lines 50 years of change
Railways to Victory 1944-46
Return to Blaenau 1970-82
SECR Centenary album
Talyllyn 50 years of change
Wareham to Swanage 50 years of change
Yeovil 50 years of change

LONDON SUBURBAN RAILWAYS

Caterham and Tattenham Corner
Charing Cross to Dartford
Clapham Jn. to Beckenham Jn.
Crystal Palace (HL) & Catford Loop
East London Line
Finsbury Park to Alexandra Palace
Holborn Viaduct to Lewisham
Kingston and Hounslow Loops
Lewisham to Dartford
Liverpool Street to Chingford
London Bridge to Addiscombe
Mitcham Junction Lines
North London Line
South London Line
West Croydon to Epsom
West London Line
Willesden Junction to Richmond
Wimbledon to Beckenham
Wimbledon to Epsom

STEAMING THROUGH

Steaming through Cornwall
Steaming through the Isle of Wight
Steaming through Kent
Steaming through West Hants

TRAMWAY CLASSICS

Aldgate & Stepney Tramways
Barnet & Finchley Tramways
Bath Tramways
Brighton's Tramways
Bristol's Tramways
Burton & Ashby Tramways
Camberwell & W.Norwood Tramways
Clapham & Streatham Tramways
Croydon's Tramways
Dover's Tramways
East Ham & West Ham Tramways
Edgware and Willesden Tramways
Eltham & Woolwich Tramways
Embankment & Waterloo Tramways
Exeter & Taunton Tramways
Fulwell - Home to Trams, Trolleys and Buses
Great Yarmouth Tramways
Greenwich & Dartford Tramways
Hammersmith & Hounslow Tramways
Hampstead & Highgate Tramways
Hastings Tramways
Holborn & Finsbury Tramways
Ilford & Barking Tramways
Kingston & Wimbledon Tramways
Lewisham & Catford Tramways
Liverpool Tramways 1. Eastern Routes
Liverpool Tramways 2. Southern Routes
Liverpool Tramways 3. Northern Routes
Maidstone & Chatham Tramways
Margate to Ramsgate
North Kent Tramways
Norwich Tramways
Reading Tramways
Seaton & Eastbourne Tramways
Shepherds Bush & Uxbridge Tramways
Southend-on-sea Tramways
South London Line Tramways 1903-33
Southwark & Deptford Tramways
Stamford Hill Tramways
Twickenham & Kingston Tramways
Victoria & Lambeth Tramways
Waltham Cross & Edmonton Tramways
Walthamstow & Leyton Tramways
Wandsworth & Battersea Tramways

TROLLEYBUS CLASSICS

Bradford Trolleybuses
Croydon Trolleybuses
Derby Trolleybuses
Hastings Trolleybuses
Huddersfield Trolleybuses
Maidstone Trolleybuses
Portsmouth Trolleybuses
Reading Trolleybuses

WATERWAY ALBUMS

Kent and East Sussex Waterways
London to Portsmouth Waterway
West Sussex Waterways

MILITARY BOOKS

Battle over Portsmouth
Battle over Sussex 1940
Blitz over Sussex 1941-42
Bombers over Sussex 1943-45
Bognor at War
Military Defence of West Sussex
Military Signals from the South Coast
Secret Sussex Resistance
Surrey Home Guard

OTHER RAILWAY BOOKS

Index to Middleton Press Stations
Industrial Railways of the South-East
South Eastern & Chatham Railways
London Chatham & Dover Railway
London Termini - Past and Proposed
War on the Line (SR 1939-45)